John L. Mac...

with
Hindsight

Charles Mortimer

*A lifetime in harmony with cars,
bikes and motorsport.*

First Published by Richard Netherwood Limited

Copyright © Charles Mortimer 1991.

ISBN 1 872 955 04 5

Designed by Richard Netherwood Limited
Typeset in Garamond by 'Word Up', Huddersfield.
Printed in Yugoslavia by Gorenjski Tisk.
Published in Great Britain by Richard Netherwood Limited.

Foreword

I first met Charles Mortimer in 1946, when motoring competition restarted after the war years, but I had seen him racing before the war, so I knew of his competition career long before our first meeting at Gransden Lodge. While still at school I had become an Alta car fan, though many of my friends were ERA fans, so consequently anyone who drove an Alta was a hero and I well remember seeing Charles at the Lewes speed trials driving Robin Jackson's dark green 1½-litre Alta. He was also a familiar figure to me at Brooklands in 1939, when I was working as a mechanic on an Alta, and he was driving his red "two-three" Bugatti and a blue MG.

For the past 44 years our paths have crossed frequently, in Charles' post-war motor racing days; during his motor trade days; at the time when he was sponsoring motorcycle riders; at his motorcycle racing School; right through to his life as a dealer in motoring books and memorabilia. About the only time I got out of touch with CKM was when he disappeared down into the West Country to run a pub!

All these things Charles writes about, and many more, in the following pages with an easy-going, happy-go-lucky approach to whatever he has done, enjoying himself to the full and accomplishing much in the pursuit of pleasure, business, dealings and a complete enjoyment of life in all its aspects.

Having read the manuscript of this book I felt I was reading my own biography, for I seem to have followed the Charles Mortimer way of life in many ways, but some ten years behind him. The early love of motor bikes, which has never diminished, a passion for motor racing in all its forms, the essential principle that whatever we do has to give pleasure and be enjoyable. About the only way I haven't followed Charles is in his love of "dealing". I have never been able to sell anything for a profit and am reluctant to buy anything, even from myself!

I am very pleased to be able to pen the foreword to this book as it is a total reflection of my idea of having a good life and enjoying every minute of it, and I hope you, the reader, enjoy it as much as I did.

Crondall, Hampshire, 1990   Denis Jenkinson

Acknowledgement

Thanks:-

To my daughter Pippa who together with Marcus Chambers put me in touch with my publishers.

To my publishers for their enthusiasm at every stage of production.

To Denis Jenkinson for agreeing to write the foreword.

To Geoff Goddard for his help with the photographs.

Contents

The Bug Bites

Meccano was the start, and the year circa 1921. The month either December, or February, my eighth birthday. One could build a better, stronger, and more operational model car with a Meccano set than any tinplate horror that could be bought — a car that, when powered with a Meccano clockwork motor, could start, stop, steer and which had a crownwheel and pinion rear axle. Later, my life's work had a gearbox added and, later still, a second engine to transform it into a World Land Speed contender. Finally, a rocket — but more of that in due course.

For me that was the start of motoring, eclipsing my previous obsession for steam in the shape of road-going traction engines and steam wagons — and even railways. This, in a way, was strange because my paternal grandfather was then a Director of the Great Western Railway, the most prestigious of them all, and one of my earliest recollections was a ride on the footplate of a Great Western 'Castle' class locomotive — not a long ride but a memorable one and by night, all the way in reverse from the engine shed to back down and couple to a night express for South Wales leaving from Paddington. My recollections of that were the vast size of the 'Castle' as seen from the footplate, the heat and brightness of the fire in contrast to the biting cold a yard or two away from it, the skill of the 'couple up' and my grandfather who took me, knowing both driver and fireman by their Christian names. With their obvious regard for him and their great kindness to me, I was rather more than proud. But I did not so much enjoy being lifted down from the platform on to the track after the 'couple up' to be shown the technique by the fireman; it was altogether too dark, cold and inhospitable down there!

In the sense that they had always had a car, my parents were early motorists — but it went no further than that. Their first, a wedding present from my grandfather who had previously promised them a new Panhard, turned out to be his own well-worn Cadillac, his first sight of the Panhard changing his mind as well as saving him money. From my mother's later description the Cadillac was first, last and always a nightmare though she herself never drove. To her a car was transport only — nothing more. Initially they had no chauffeur so that with my dear old father solely in charge I was surprised to hear that they ever set out to go anywhere — but they did, and obviously every trip was more awful than the previous one. Our house, 'Royston Chase' stood in the centre of a large garden, in deep country and within a hundred yards of the Brooklands Track's Byfleet banking and though I was born there in February 1913, on the day that Percy Lambert first covered 100 miles in one hour on the track, its presence was never once mentioned during the time we lived there. Years later my mother told me that they had bought the house not only for the lovely and happy house it was but also because the presence of the track had caused Byfleet properties, and 'Royston Chase' in particular, to plummet pricewise.

In retrospect, I suppose that my father was an unusual man even for those days. A man of the highest principles, always kind and courteous, he was I think, lazy and a dreamer. He must have had a good brain to have become a barrister but the 'rub' was that he never once accepted a brief. The family, thanks largely to my mother, revolved round his interests which were shooting, stamp, butterfly and bee collecting and painting sunsets in oil. His various collections were quite magnificent. So were his oil paintings, which often as not he destroyed on the following day. Once, when he asked me what I would like for Christmas, I surprised him by saying, truthfully, that more than anything else, I would like a painting of sunset of my grandfather's house, 'Wigmore' shown from across its lake (where I spent countless happy hours fishing). It was not done the next day, because the sunset was somehow not beautiful enough, but the day after that. I still have it and love it. Holidays were mostly the standard pattern — with a difference. We had a chauffeur by that time but our holiday journeys to the seaside were made by train while the chauffeur had his holiday elsewhere at the same time. Always we had to go somewhere where a rare butterfly or bee was known to flutter and always places renowned for their sunsets. The result of this, of course was that my mother, sister and I made our own plans, and in our own way, thoroughly enjoyed the holidays.

One produced an absolutely marvellous episode, a holiday in Barton, in the New Forest, this time in search of a particular rare bee. Staying at the same small hotel were a lovely family, the Evans — dad, mum, and two boys of about my age, Adrian and Nicholas, with whom I used to go on long bike trips. The fun started one evening when my father was showing them his bee collection, all dead of course and beautifully set with tiny pins on long white paper covered cork strips in display cases. Both were obviously gripped and within days bikes were abandoned in favour of collecting nets and the rest of the paraphernalia. Each day, my father advised them where to go and what species to look out for, meeting again in the evening and comparing their prizes. There was a big stir one evening when they displayed a species among their catch that my father had never seen, again beautifully set with all the others. A new species, hitherto unknown, of British Bee! They were ecstatic! No collecting next day. My father was off to the Natural History Museum in London, returning that evening triumphant with the news that, subject to confirmation, this was indeed the case. But during our long bike ride that day Adrian and Nicholas told me the truth — that they had, in fact, built up a 'composite' bee from the body of one species, the head of another, legs and wings of another, so beautifully that even the master was deceived and, to some extent, the Museum as well. But two days later a letter from London revealed the truth, and to his credit, my father enjoyed the joke as much as anyone.

Initially, I was too young to have known the Cadillac which was only a two-seater anyway. My first recollection was of its successor, a large and stately Fiat Landaulette, driven by a chauffeur-handyman named Burrage who had recently lost his job as a groom, due to the death of his employer. Seeing the light, he had sensibly taken a course in 'automobilism'. He drove the car on the rare occasions it went out, polished the bodywork and brass ceaselessly, drove and looked after the pony, 'Lizzie' who pulled the vast lawn mower and did many other things as well. I never saw him raise the bonnet of the Fiat except to

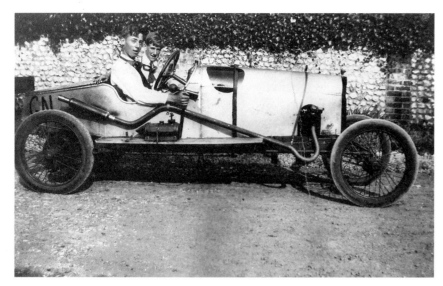

'Boy's Racer' A very sporting chain drive G.N. 'special' bought for £4 and greatly enjoyed.

polish the brass induction pipe and some smaller copper ones, or undertake even rudimentary maintenance, but the Fiat never once gave trouble — and Burrage got the credit.

He became a firm friend and, to some extent, my mentor, first showing me exactly how to drive and why one made the motions so that, quite soon, I had a fairly good idea of how and when to do what — and why, though it was years later that I first drove — and then not with him.

Meanwhile, when I was nine I was sent to boarding school in the nearby countryside — and hated it. I'd been there a year when one of the masters started an affair with the Headmaster's wife and the school closed. After a long summer holiday I was despatched to a 'crammer' down in Devon run by a clergyman and his wife — better than the first, but it was still home that I loved. In 1927 I scraped into Radley, literally and by virtue of the fact that I was said to have had a lovely singing voice which had broken by the time I arrived at Radley, to the disgust of the Precentor who sought a useful addition to the Choir, and later to the disgust of my Housemaster who discovered that he'd inherited not only a dunce but one not

too keen on cricket.

By then, I had made my first visit to Brooklands, seen the Delages win the 1926 **Grand Prix at the same time as frying their** drivers' feet, seen the Talbot's front axle break in half and Campbell's Bugatti, the only car still running happily, finish second, and decided, once and for all, what I wanted to do in life regardless of all the obstacles I would have to surmount. That day set the course of my life. September 3rd 1939 changed it, though, by that time I had had six enjoyable and quite successful years of racing at Brooklands on two wheels and also four of quite successful racing on four, mostly on Brough Superior, Norton, MG, Bugatti and Alta.

But a lot was to happen before I got to Brooklands as a resident competitor. Nearly six years as a spectator for one thing, during which I realised that the big problem towards becoming a racing driver was expense. Quite quickly, though, it dawned on me that one way would be to start racing with bikes, graduating to cars later. I became interested in bikes and in the summer of 1927 bought my first one — without parental consent and with my own money — for the vast sum of £4. I bought it locally and within days found that I was regarded as the local 'Rothschild'. It was a good bike, a Douglas, but the 'right' price for it would have been £1. Yes, in 1927 that was the price of a ten or twelve year old bike in good running order — and there was no shortage of them. It was my first setback, but I learned a lot, not only from the deal itself, but from the bike also. By then we had moved from Byfleet to Dorking. Burrage and the Fiat had gone, the latter being replaced by an open tourer Austin 'Twenty' and the former by Woodham.

Woodham and the Austin were a much faster combination than Burrage and the Fiat. True, the Fiat had done very few long journeys. Byfleet to West Byfleet — two miles each way — was the norm and a forty mile trip was a long one. But one could never recall seeing the speedometer showing much above forty miles an hour on the Fiat or much below that on the Austin. And good friend as Burrage had been, Woodham was younger, with more mechanical knowledge and, therefore, better.

Our move from Byfleet to Dorking still stirs the memory, being the last I ever saw undertaken by steam. Much shouting and clouds of steam revealed a huge, box-bodied Foden steam wagon pushing its equally large box trailer up the drive before uncoupling, proceeding down the drive on its own, turning in the main road and reversing back to the front door ready to couple up again when loaded. The load-up took all day, the wagon still in steam so that every time the fire was fuelled, clouds of black acrid smoke drifted up and into the windows of the house, much to my mother's alarm. As a sideline, the monster periodically decanted into the drive about fifteen or twenty gallons of boiling water which mixed nicely with ash lying there from the fire grate. Asking the reason for this, I was told by the driver that she 'tended to prime' when not steaming. Great stuff, all of it!

Neither my sister or I had seen much of my mother during the run up to the move. Poor love, she must have organised it virtually single-handed, for my father continued to go shooting regularly and painting sunsets each evening. But when we arrived at Dorking, she had already managed, somehow, to ensure that our new house had atmosphere and was already 'a home' so that by the time the removal cortège had unloaded and departed and the furniture was 'in situ' we felt as though we had lived there for years. The house, quite large, was on the outskirts of the town, approached by a private, circular road in which were one or two other houses of about the same size. It had a smaller garden than the one we had left but a larger total acreage because there was quite a large area of woodland.

Two house painters were hard at work painting the outside and, in the drive, stood their transport, a Morris 30cwt truck proclaiming 'J & J Franks — Builders and Decorators' and, had I known it, the Franks brothers were to be instrumental in effecting a big change in my life. There were several outbuildings in the garden and one, furthest from the house and set within the woodland area, was allocated to me as a 'workshop'. It was when I was pushing my treasured Douglas to it that the brothers Franks suddenly showed interest, for it then transpired that they too were not only keen motorcyclists but also joint owners of a beautiful Alvis 12/50 Sports 'Ducktail' two-seater. The house painting had to proceed but every tea-break was spent discussing motorbikes and from them I learned of a supply source they knew, at which there were four or five hundred bikes for sale at prices ranging from £1 to £20. That started the big change.

Family transport took an upward surge at this stage as did our social lives. Our new neighbours, the Martineaus, were a large family and all very motor minded. Howard

An Austin Twenty of the type driven by 'Woodham' the Mortimer family chauffeur.

Martineau himself had three cars, two big Napiers, a limousine and an open tourer, and a 12/50 Alvis saloon. There were four boys, David, Guy, Dennis and Bernard, all older than I except Bernard who was my own age. I seem to recall Dennis as the only one not very motor minded but David and Guy then had Grand Prix Salmsons after having gone through the usual Morgan Three Wheeler phase.

Our big Austin Twenty had proved an absolutely marvellous car. It was, I think, the first post-war model the firm had produced with several rather ingenious innovations such as a disappearing hood and the spare wheel concealed instead of mounted on the running board or at the rear. It was roomy, completely reliable and, at that time, quite fast and, if pushed, would show an indicated 70 mph. With hindsight, I think it may have been fairly heavy on fuel for, during our first year at Dorking, it was joined by a delightful little Weyman-bodied Renault '9', it's

opposite in almost all respects except reliability. The Renault, with it's 'coal scuttle' type bonnet and 'early perpendicular' body styling was typically French, extremely slow and economical, and exuded character and personality. Many of my trips to Brooklands were made in it with Woodham driving and I think that of all the small cars of that period, it would be the one I would still like to own. Some of the Martineau 'motor magic' seemed to have rubbed off on my father for, a year or two later, when Howard Martineau replaced his Napier Limousine with a 40/50 hp Rolls Royce, the Austin departed and the Napier took its place. But not for long.

Returning from Brooklands one day, a cyclist shot out from a side turning, causing maximum braking from its rear wheels only, and transmission handbrake. The cyclist emerged unscathed but the strain on the crownwheel and pinion of the Napier was too much. It succumbed with a mighty crash and the ensuing bill for repairs brought about the car's departure, and replacement with a brand new Morris Isis Six saloon, quite a satisfactory car in its way though it seemed rather to lack charisma. But with Woodham's connivance — and without my father's knowledge — it was on the Isis that I did most of my early driving, finally seeking official permission and recognition which was granted provided I underwent a course of driving lessons to which I gladly agreed. The lessons were given by Mr. Wallen, manager of the Dorking Motor Company who, of course, unaware of the distance I'd already driven, put me through the whole process and delighted dear old Dad by telling him that in all his experience of teaching, he'd never come across a more apt and intelligent pupil or one able to grasp every aspect — a natural driver in fact!

But back, now, to the Franks Bros. Confirming that the price I had paid for the Douglas was 'well over the top', Jack and Joe Franks then mounted an intensive campaign to liquidate it, effecting a sale at the price I'd paid within a week, greatly to my, and their, surprise and, of course, restoring me to liquidity and, so they promised, in a much better position to buy again. Not only that, but they promised, on the following Sunday, to take me down to their 'Aladdin's Cave' in Sussex.

To this day I recall the journey down and back in the Alvis, with Jack driving on the way out and Joe on the run homeward. Nor shall I ever forget the scene when we got there — a small roadside, two-pump filling station set at the edge of a ten or twelve acre field with, in the centre, a vast two-storey Nissen type building packed with motor bikes; the outside area was a forest of earlier ones, priced between £1 and £4, the ground floor of the building held machines from £5 to £9 and, on top, the 'cream' between £10 and £20. Only a full day spent there would suffice and the day it was that we spent, lunching in the packed, quite large cafe on bacon and eggs and tea — 'all in' set price a shilling (five pence) a head.

I recall discussing our plan of action during lunch and finding that our total 'investable' capital was £14, a fiver from each Franks plus my £4 which meant that we could buy, even from the top floor, with quite a good margin or get bulk for our money lower down. At the end of the day I was the owner of an early transverse ABC with overhead valves, Jack a 'four valve' Rudge and Joe an overhead valve P & M Panther. By the end of the day, the plan was laid for a 'threesome' partnership. They would collect the bikes with their Morris after work, the bikes would go to my 'workshop' where I would 'go to town' on them, first by cleaning and smartening them generally after which we would have the next 'board meeting' — for we had managed to get all three running without actually riding them, due to the dense traffic congestion in the field!

That was the start, not only of an honourable and successful partnership but also of my life spent in dealing. Not all the problems of such a partnership were there, for the usual problems of a dealer are either too much stock and not enough capital with which to buy or vice versa — and thanks to our wonderful supply position, we never suffered from the latter. Though it might have turned out differently, I was in league with two of the most straightforward and honourable men I ever knew and as time went on, our links became closer. At the time I met them, both were 'going steady' with two local young ladies, sisters, and they, in turn, became the nucleus of our domestic staff, as parlour maid and housemaid, staying with us until we left the house twelve years later. Not only that but they found us a marvellous cook who also stayed until we left.

Our part time business went from strength

to strength. It had to be part time because the Franks had their own business to run, and I was only at home for the school holidays, and there were, of course, other things to do. I was making regular visits to Brooklands, usually by push bike, my main means of transport at that stage.

Initially, I went to the motor bike and smaller car race meetings which were cheaper but, finding that the track was open on non-race days at almost no charge, I switched to those. Far, far better because there was always something happening on those days, and famous racing people around. The journey from Dorking was around twenty miles and, in the summer and Easter holidays I used to leave home not later than six in the morning, stopping at the White Lion at Cobham for breakfast and arriving at the track around nine. That way I became on Christian name terms with many of the famous, which helped a lot later on. Any tiredness I might have had vanished within half an hour of getting home and, with very little traffic on the road, those rides were absolutely glorious. Now and again well-known drivers would spot me en route and stop, throwing my bike into the back of their 30/98 Vauxhall or Bentley, halving my journey time — and more than once I arrived with it slung across the tail of a Boulogne Frazer Nash.

The initial problem of marketing our motorbike stock was quickly solved. Local newspaper advertising was turned down on account of expense but in those days almost all small shops and some Post Offices had little notice boards on which you could put quite a large advertisement for two pence per week — and this worked well.

It seemed a good idea to tell my mother what was going on though I felt sure she had some idea anyway. She did, of course and so did my father who, far from opposing it, had been quite in favour so long as the machines were not ridden and so long as it

didn't get too big and intrude on our lives. I had ridden all of them at various times when he was out — untaxed, with no driving licence or, of course, insurance which was not complusory in those days — and only on the 'private' road. On one occasion I arrived back, on a big twin Zenith, to find the local policeman awaiting me, but it turned out that he was a friend of Jack and Joe and had been 'tipped off' by them as he, too was a motorcyclist — and later made more than one purchase from us. Some of the machines were rather noisy and the only advice he gave me was to make friends with the owners of other houses on the road so that if there were to be complaints, they wouldn't go direct to 'the station'. I did this, taking it a bit further and always being available if any of the neighbours' cars wouldn't start — which did happen from time to time! During the time we did all this, numerous machines passed through our hands including some really lovely ones because, of course, as our finances improved, so did the quality of the 'stock'.

But all good things come to an end. I left Radley in 1930 with some regret, for I had been happier there than at either of my prep schools. There had been some aspects that I hadn't enjoyed, such as compulsory cold baths all the year round at 6.30 each morning, but in those days the school was far more up-to-date and progressive than its competitors and on the whole it was a happy period and I made some good friends.

I knew that, ere long, my father would be talking with me about the future and, forestalling him, I raised it quite soon. I realised, of course that to put forward the 'racing motorist' idea alone would be to court disaster so I put it indirectly, saying that though this was ultimately what I wanted to do, I realised that I would first need more technical knowledge and had a friend who had said he would take me on as an apprentice — at no premium. This was true, for Henry Nash, the local Norton and New Imperial agent, had said so. But my father's counter of apprenticeship to Rolls Royce, though more prestigious, was just as unacceptable to me as my idea was to him, and in the end I was left to make another suggestion.

Finally, dear old Brooklands solved the problem for, at one of the Easter Bank Holiday meetings, the programme carried a full-page advertisement of the College of Automobile Engineering in Chelsea, and having been shown its prospectus my father agreed willingly. A month or two later I found myself in 'digs' in Notting Hill Gate and a pupil of the College at which I stayed until my father's death in 1932. I did learn a lot there but had I worked harder could have learned more. But Brooklands was only forty minutes from London by train and many were the days when I played truant to go there, nearly always finding that, next week, there were long distance records, car or bike, being attempted which I felt I ought to see.

I had a marvellous landlady in whom I always confided regarding my Brooklands sorties and whenever I was down there I would 'phone her just to check that there had been no 'phone calls from home. On one of these occasions I found here upset and worried for my mother had 'phoned to say that my father was seriously ill and my presence at home was urgently required. A bus from Weybridge to Leatherhead followed by another from Leatherhead to Dorking got me home within the hour, for which I was thankful because he died early next morning.

I adored and admired my mother and realised that it was now up to me to help her in every way I could. Time eased the blow. Initially, so as to be available to help if needed, I apprenticed myself to the local Daimler and Lanchester agents, learned more and enjoyed it. There were some quaint customs in those days. Nearly every garage had a taxi and ours was a vast Austin Twenty. So as not to waste the time of the skilled fitters it was the apprentice's job to drive it — a pearl of a job, for tips frequently came one's way. My first long run with the Austin was to take two elderly alcoholic ladies from Dorking to Warnes Hotel at Worthing where they wined and dined before returning. The job was done on an hourly basis so that their main concern was to waste as little time travelling as possible. That, of course, was no problem and fast as we went on the outward run, we went far faster on the return when my passengers rolled about in the back content with the best fare that Warnes could supply. After our first trip they would have no one but me to drive them, telling the manager that they found my driving 'so skilled and careful'. Despite our speed, the overall time taken was the same, the balance of time being spent in the bar before their lunch.

Another 'apprentice' task was the collection of new Daimler and Lanchester cars from the Midlands. This also was done against the clock because it was just, and only just, possible to collect two cars in one day with some luck and as little hard driving as possible. Leaving Dorking at five o'clock in the morning, one took the train to London, Underground from Victoria to Euston and then train to the Midlands. If one's car was ready, one was winning. New cars, of course, they varied in 'tightness', so one had to be careful with one that had a tight engine. Thirty miles an hour was the recommended maximum but much more was necessary to maintain the schedule. No motorways, of course, and roads packed with slow moving 'heavies', so passing was more of a headache than straightforward cruising. We became very skilled at spotting the 'tight' ones, usually before leaving the city limits, and it was easier to maintain the schedule with a Lanchester 'Twenty' than with a 'Ten'. And as it was only the first col-

Mrs Mortimer presented her son Charles with his first new car, a 1933 Austin Ten which he kept for years as reliable everyday transport.

lection that had to be done against time one always hoped to be able to collect a bigger horsepower car first. Once one had collected the second there was really no rush as one had a key to the works when one finally got home. Later one would see all these cars religiously run in by the new owners at 30 miles an hour maximum!

After a time, it was suggested that I should join the Sales Department which seemed great until I discovered that the job was to be knocking on doors and touting for business, not only for sales but also the service department. I stuck this for a month and hated it, asked for my service job back,

was refused and left.

I felt I had reached the point at which I ought to be working at Brooklands but was still concerned about my mother. As always, she was marvellous about it, not only agreeing, but, as well, making me a present of my first car, a brand new 1933 Austin Ten, a wonderful little car, which despite owning others later, I kept for years. The scaled-up edition of the world famous 'Seven', I always thought it an infinitely better car — and it never let me down, even when towing a trailer carrrying two or even three racing bikes. For some reason I never discovered, my mother, while agreeing to

Jock Forbes on Charles' 250 Excelsior at Governors' Bridge in the 1938 Manx Grand Prix. Jock finished sixth.

my racing motor bikes at Brooklands, was terrified about racing in the Isle of Man. To promise her not to do so was no problem at the time even though it did become one later. When the time came I sounded her out again but she still felt the same so I later went to the Island looking after my T.T. machines which Jock Forbes rode for me.

The year prior to my father's death had been a difficult one for by then I had, in fact, taken premises at Brooklands, dealing in almost anything except cars during holidays from the College. The term 'premises' is, in retrospect, rather a laugh. I rented a tiny shed, the smallest available floor space eight feet by ten, under the Finishing Straight Grandstand, annual rent £10! Payable half yearly also!

Though the Austin was my first new car, I had owned one other previously. At the time, I was an ardent scanner of all advertise-ments offering motorbikes or cars for sale and one day spotted a 1921 two seater G.N. for sale, quite locally and priced at £4, I didn't know what a G.N. looked like at the time and one look at this, with its Mercedes-like 'Vee' fronted radiator was enough — and back it went to Dorking. At the time, it was the right car for me with its simplicity and quite sporting appearance allied to what seemed to me sparkling performance.

When I look back on my G.N. motoring I'm appalled at some of the chances I took. Initially, it took place on our 'private' road but the big 'Vee'-twin engine was noisy and although there were no actual complaints from our neighbours, some smiles were replaced by frowns and it wasn't long before my 'tours' were being made further afield, sometimes being accompanied by Bernard Martineau or an enthusiast schoolfriend, Ronnie Croft.

Insurance was not compulsory in those days, a driving licence was 'affordable' at five shillings and, when I got the G.N. there was still six months to run shown in the licence holder. Wings had been removed to make the car look more 'racy', a 'racing' body replaced the rather staid touring version and having seen so many runners in the 200 Mile Race at Brooklands labelled 'Special', the bonnet bore the words 'Mortimer Special', about as big a 'give-away' as one could wish for. Main road traffic was probably one tenth of what it is today and side roads carried virtually nothing, so it was to the side roads we went. There were no mobile police, the only versions being either on foot or push bike and if one met the latter when rounding a sharp bend, the technique was to put the right foot down and motor hard till out of sight or sound. If one was less fortunate and encountered one at the far end of a long straight, it meant braking and full right lock on full power and home as quickly as possible. What we really dreaded was a breakdown but strangely it never came. Motorbikes on the road worried my mother — and how right she was. For that reason alone I did practically no road riding and must, I suppose, have been the only Brooklands rider to have lined up to start in his first race never having ridden further than up and down the drive or on the private road.

The gift of the Austin Ten was manna from heaven and, initially it was enough just to drive in it further and further afield in the knowledge that it was not only reliable but also 'legal'. That phase ended with the thought that, great as it was, I was doing no work and ought now to to get things moving at Brooklands, so one very cold December morning I drove to the track, unlocked the door of my 'premises' in the Paddock and sat down to make a plan. Incredibly, without the company of the Franks brothers I felt almost at a loss to know how to start. That really was rather strange because whenever we were together as a threesome each had always vied with the others on ideas to expand 'the business'. I sat for some time with the doors closed, getting colder and colder and more and more frustrated, before going up to the canteen for a cup of coffee. The problem seemed to be twofold, first that thriving as our business had been, it was dealing in 'bangers' which, in my new environment, was really quite out of the question. Secondly, I had only limited capital and far too little technical knowledge — and none at all concerning racing machinery. The thing began to clarify as I sipped my coffee. I had dealt quite successfully and learned a lot from Jack and Joe so must continue to do two things, the first to be a dealer and the second a racing motor cyclist, preferably both simultaneously. But capital was the problem so dealing obviously had to come first. Had I known it, the solutions to both problems were to come quite quickly, the major one the very next day.

One Thing at a Time

December was the 'dead' part of the year where Brooklands was concerned but at the last bike meeting of the year, while strolling round the paddock, I'd passed the door of a Brooklands rider very well known even then. Eric Fernihough had been works rider for Excelsiors that year and outside his premises stood a blackboard offering all his machines for sale. Most were priced between £50 and £80 — a lot of money in those days but one, a 175cc E.F. JAP, was priced at £15 and knocking on the door I asked to see it. Eric couldn't have been friendlier — he always was when a deal was in the offing. But the snag was that the machine wasn't there but down at his garage at Southampton. He was coming up to Brooklands in a month's time however and if I could wait, would bring it up then. I certainly could and though I didn't say so at the time, a month would give me more time to amass finance. Eric didn't know that, of course. And what I didn't know was that though he had the components to build such a machine, that was all he had at the time of that meeting. The bike which bore his initials was, in a sense his brainchild — to be built from odd bits and pieces lying around. No one but Eric could have thought of it. At the time I had thought it must be just another marketable banger despite his graphic description and assurance that it was a genuine racing machine in mint condition. I couldn't understand it — but we did the deal — deferred payment and delivery, within a month or two.

When I first saw that machine, I knew that despite its one big snag, it was going to be the one I would ride when the next season opened. All its components were mint and nearly new — but all were obsolete. The engine consisted of the crankcase of a 250cc side valve JAP touring engine, the cylinder was one of a pair from an early vertical overhead valve experimental twin, the frame was Montgomery and the forks Triumph. But Eric had forgotten to mention one thing — that the drive from the two-speed Albion gearbox to the rear wheel was by belt, not chain, and since a belt driven bike hadn't competed at Brooklands for the previous ten years, it had never occurred to me to ask! He hadn't misrepresented it — I just hadn't asked. But shocked as I was, I knew that it was the bike that would get me started at Brooklands — and it did.

From that cold December day onwards, things began to move. Noticing that most 'racers' had their names painted on the doors of their premises I emblazoned mine with 'Charles Mortimer. Racing Machines and Equipment Bought, Sold and Exchanged' and this did more than anything to get things moving, for behind the scenes the Brooklands Paddock was a dealer's paradise. Vendors were the first to arrive. At that time almost no one had money but everyone had something to sell. Initially, and fortunately, no one asked me to maintain a machine but once the season started and even before that, one thing led to another and there were other sources of income mostly gleaned in

First racing bike. Bought unseen from Eric Fernihough who then proceeded to cobble it together from various bits and called it an 'E.F.' The last belt driven bike to race at Brooklands.

the canteen mid-morning and at lunchtime. Someone told me about a firm called Aldridges in London who held a weekly auction of mainly big horsepower cars which usually sold very very cheaply. That was understandable because, at tht time, everyone was switching from big to small cars. But I went and was staggered to find what beautiful big cars could be bought for almost no money. I felt that if big cars could be sold at all, it must be possible to sell them at Brooklands: I bought a Chrysler '65' two-seater the following week and sold it within a fortnight so others followed.

Though nobody told me, I found out that a stop-watch was a good investment. Some paddock tenants spent days timing cars practising prior to a race meeting so that, after having looked at handicaps in the programme they probably knew the likely

winners of eight out of ten races. Though I hadn't realised it till then, my shed was ideal for that. I only had to look out of the window to 'clock' them as they went onto the Home Banking — and 'collect' from the bookmakers on Race Day!

But it wasn't long before I began to realise that, with hindsight, I had started my 'business' at the wrong time, trading in the wrong sort of thing and, in a sense, at the wrong place. The time, when the world trade recession was at its peak, was certainly wrong, and with literally no passing trade, the Brooklands paddock was far from ideal. But that was where I wanted to be and was determined to remain.

I started some 'new' lines. Many of the paddock sheds housed racing cars owned by wealthy drivers and maintained by single mechanics who, from time to time, required help in the form of muscle and another pair of hands when removing or replacing an engine as well as for other chores such as collecting spare parts, sometimes from Weybridge station, sometimes from London but quite often from much further afield. So, having cast the word around that I was always 'available' to help at crisis times, I quickly became a 'much in demand' additional 'pair of hands', learning quite a lot in the process — particularly that motor racing really is a series of leaps from one crisis to the next. I also became proficient at either end of a tow rope, which made me more in demand, and reasonably good at racing car assemblies, including engines, all of which was a help when, later, I started racing other bikes, particularly Nortons. I aimed, also, at getting a reputation for dependability, that is to say always doing what I'd said I would do, always being there on or before time and, when making long or short journeys, always being able to forecast how long they would take, subject to not being let down 'at the other end'.

The only times when I wasn't 'available' were for the two or three days before meetings where programmes consisted of a series of short handicap races which were the only events on which I betted. Long races were much too open — anything could happen in an event like, say, the B.R.D.C. '500' and even casual spectators could often pick winners of scratch races even though it wouldn't do them much good because the bookmakers knew as well — and shortened their odds accordingly. But for some reason, the winners of short handicaps usually surprised the less well informed.

To become a professional punter needed some time and a little inside knowledge. I used to take my little Austin to a remote point on the track where the Railway Straight joined with the start of the Byfleet banking, armed with at least one good stop-watch, plenty of food and drink, pens,

pencils and masses of paper and park where neither the public nor drivers circulating could spot us. By the end of the two days one knew exactly the best lap time of every car and driver competing. Armed with the programme of the meeting one then dealt with the problem race by race. Taking the first race one jotted down the best recorded lap time of each runner, then scanned the field for a runner, or maybe more than one, a regular competitor in short handicaps whose lap time never varied — and usually there were more than one. Say, for instance that the chap always lapped at 110 mph meeting after meeting: you just worked the result out based on the virtual certainty that he'd do so again. With the Brooklands Lap Speed table you could then work out from the handicap times for the race in order to dead heat with him, whether each of the others couldn't or whether they could do better. If worse, they weren't in the hunt. If better, it was just a question of looking through your notes to find whose lap times were 'up' on their handicaps and selecting as 'winner' the one with the biggest improvement.

That wasn't quite all though. One sometimes found more than one of the 'improvers' dead heating making it necessary to get more information which could come either from their mechanics, whom one probably knew anyway, or via the Club bar at the end of the day, from the mouths of the runners themselves! But with the information you had on the race, you certainly knew more of everyone's chances than the drivers themselves and often more than their mechanics as well, and it quite often happened that, in the bar, one would hear drivers quite convinced that they were winners next day, whereas, barring accidents which seldom happened in short handicaps, one knew perfectly well that they weren't. The bookmakers were not fools. They soon got to know one, so money had to be placed with them via friends of whom, fortunately, there were plenty and it was a poor day when one didn't pick winners of six out of eight races — it quite often used to be eight of of eight. Years later I restarted my 'professional punting' when the bookies re-appeared at Goodwood car meetings, sometimes in league with my old friend George Abecassis.

The E.F. JAP took me through my first season of racing, followed by a 250cc New Henly JAP and a best outer circuit lap time of 85 mph. In 1933 both with no wins but one or two 'seconds' and 'thirds' and part way through the season, a 350cc overhead camshaft Chater Lea in both Solo and Sidecar events. Best solo lap with that was just over 90 and, with sidecar, slightly better than 80mph.

Though at this point I was really enjoying the racing and knew what I wanted to do where the racing was concerned, I was enjoying not only my car dealing but also the ownership, even if only temporary, of the cars in which I was trading. I did want to get a British Motorcycle Club's 'Gold Star' for an outer circuit lap at over 100mph and a few wins as opposed to 'seconds' and 'thirds' — and I knew that, in the end, I would sooner or later have to race cars at Brooklands. I now knew enough about Brooklands to realise that, with the, even then, rather primitive bike suspension we had, a three figure lap must be quite an experience, particularly on the bankings and with that in mind, I made a wrong choice.

I bought a 'big twin', a 1000cc Brough Superior, the theory being that with that amount of power I would be able to 'cruise' round the bankings and 'gun it' at the Fork and down the Railway straight. How wrong! Later, on 'five hundreds', I covered literally

Riding the rather ancient but effective 350cc Chater Lea (number 19) in company with E.G. Bishop. In sidecar form it was also used to give various helpers and friends passenger rides as a sort of reward.

hundreds of three-figure laps almost as routine. The memory of the same speed on the '1000' still remains. It was hard work and very 'hairy' by comparison! It finally excelled itself when practising one Thursday for the B.M.C.R.C. Cup Day meeting on the following Saturday. Ted Baragwaneth, to all intents and purposes Brough's Works rider, had been doing some work on the front end to try to improve the handling which initially seemed so much improved on the first lap that, on lap two, I decided to keep it on 'full song' all the way round. Surprisingly, it was fractious crossing the Fork and seemed worse when running onto the Members Banking so, in an effort to placate it, I let it run high all the way round the banking. Coming off, it hit the big bump above the River Wey with a wallop, landing badly and becoming quite uncontrollable — the biggest fright I'd ever had with a bike. Even while slowing down it was awful, weaving from one way to the other, which wasn't surprising because when we did at last grind to a halt I found that the front down-tube of the frame had broken so badly that there was a three-inch gap between the top of the tube and the steering-head lug. To make matters worse my timekeeper, Johnny Waite came motoring up, face wreathed in smiles, with the news that the average for lap two had been just over a hundred and six, seven miles an hour better than the previous best, meaning that, if we ran, the race would be 'in the bag'.

Back in the paddock, I rang George Brough at the works in Nottingham. Dear George — just his sort of problem. "Don't worry, boy. Take the wheels out. Take the front passenger seat out of the car, remove the forks if you have to but leave the engine in — and come straight up. We'll hang on if you're not here by closing time. It won't take more than two hours at the most and you can have a meal while we're doing it and then set off home".

Not many like him these days and it all went perfectly. Though the works had closed when I arrived at seven that evening, there he was with his foreman, Ike Webb, and together they did it — and stood me food and drink. "So you think the old thing might pull it off on Saturday, do you? Well then, I'd better come down — and we'll fleece the Bookies". Luckily, it did work out that way with a best lap of 105.74 and an average for the race of 100.82.

Many riders of that era had their race bikes permanently for sale so, though it took a little time to sell, the Brough then became an item of stock — having by then, had a few laps on a Manx Norton, I knew for the first time exactly where I was going in 1935. But it was a little time before, with one 500cc cylinder, I could better the Brough's Gold Star lap with two.

By now, I was very busy, mainly with matters unconnected with racing but with making money. When, in the early 1930's, I first became a 'resident', that is to say someone who had premises and worked there all the year round, the population consisted of 'residents', regular visitors, those who came nearly every day throughout the season, and a third group who never missed a car meeting. At that time *the* 'residents' were Thompson and Taylor, whose premises were the largest and oldest established as builders and maintainers of racing cars whose clients were mostly the 'cream' of racing motorists, wealthy and usually competing at all big and some smaller meetings. Their premises were largest and situated over at the aerodrome area on the Byfleet side. 'T & T's were a legend and a book could and should have been written of their history.

Next, in order of seniority, R. R. Jackson Ltd. with premises, extremely well equipped, in the Paddock. Whereas T & Ts, who had operated from the 1920's, had the 'Crème de la Crème' of clients, among

whom were Sir Malcolm Campbell and John Cobb. Robin Jackson at first catered for the next echelon down. He had himself been a regular competitor at the track with Morgans and MG's but was first and last a 'boffin' and more interested in the technical side than in competing. I recall his premises being built in the early 1930's and, unlike T & Ts, he catered for both bike and car people. He built up a wonderful staff with people like Bob Hubbersty, 'Curly' Skelton and designer/technician 'Sinbad' Milledge. One of his first customers was that lovely character Robert Waddy with his tiny but successful little sprint car 'Fuzzi', a single seater, twin engined with one 500cc Speedway JAP engine mounted ahead of the driver and another astern. From the start there was a bond between Robert and 'Sinbad' both of whom were — how shall I put it — 'Bohemian', though 'Sinbad' was bearded and elegant while dear Robert usually looked as though he'd just been rescued from a long period on a desert island! Both were technically minded and original thinkers and

both friendly, happy and amusing extroverts. The 'Robinery' as it became known, grew rapidly and while still catering for the 'middle echelon' of racing motorists was also happy to cater for the often almost penniless motorcycle community.

I think that Francis Beart and Noel Pope, who later held the motorcycle Brooklands Lap Record at over 120mph, became 'residents' at about the same time as I did, though Noel might have arrived slightly later. Noel was passionately interested in racing at the track and in as many races everywhere else as he could and took on no outside business whereas Francis' business gave a service to motorcycle people only and later became very 'Norton' orientated. He had earlier apprenticed himself to Eric Fernihough who then had a garage just outside the track on the Brooklands Road. Initially, the business had been founded by Myles Rothwell and was later taken over by him.

In character, Eric Fernihough was different from all of us. A Cambridge graduate, he was really the last of the purely professional Brooklands racing motorcyclists. Brainy, serious-minded, technical and utterly dedicated, almost humourless and no fun to work with, he strove constantly for perfection — and usually found it. If one had an elusive technical problem with a bike, he was the chap to talk to — but it cost money.

The Dunlop Tyre Service Depot made up the nucleus of the Brooklands 'Residents Society' into which I had moved. Housed in a rather attractive medium-sized building known as 'The Chalet', they gave a second-to-none service to all. David McDonald, known to all as 'Dunlop Mac', was in charge with either two or three fitters depending on the likely volume of business. 'Fiddle', Mac's second-in-command, was almost always there, then came 'Reg' and the 'Lad' who really was only a lad and in the team at pressure times such as the week before the B.R.D.C. 500 Mile Race or other long distance events. 'Dunlops' as they were known, motored down in the van from London headquarters in Albany Street and were always at the track throughout the season. Perhaps I should say 'almost always', for at slack times in the season such as the beginning and end, they sometimes would stop for a pint at the 'Toby Jug' at Tolworth on the Kingston Bypass. But no matter, everyone knew where they were and an impolite message conveyed to them in the bar would always bring them down post-haste.

That really constituted the 'Residents Society' in the 1930's, though others came — and sometimes went. Then, of course, there were the competitors, most of whom were there only on race days or for a few days testing and practising prior to a meeting. Though Brooklands was really a 'classless' society a rather comic situation existed because moneywise and socially there were two groups, the upper and the lower. The upper consisted of car people

and the lower, the motorcycle people, in effect the 'Haves' and 'Have-nots'.

The comic side of this was that, sometimes each group was infiltrated by someone from the other who would always be happily accepted once he was found to be a 'good chap'. On the bike side, people in this category consisted of chaps like Jock Forbes, 'Spug' Muir and 'Crasher' White, all of whom had just come down from Cambridge University, and others like Jimmy Waite and myself. We had all been to Public schools and spoke what was then termed the King's English but once our real interest in racing was established, we were instantly accepted. The same applied among the car people and perhaps the best example concerned dear Fred Dixon who had been an enormously successful bike man since way back in the 1920's. Fred was a North Countryman, a brilliant rider and technician who called a spade a spade, had his own way of saying it, and even in his bike era, took no nonsense from anyone, duke or dustman. It was in the mid 1930's when he switched from bike racing to cars, becoming instantly successful with Rileys. Far from being awed by his new circle of competitors he made the switch in a manner scornful and, at times almost belligerent. He wasn't going to 'take any nonsense from 'em'.

At that time, Earl Howe was, I think, President of the British Racing Driver's Club and, as a good President, always took trouble to make new drivers and members welcome. Howe was and looked an earl, but earl of a previous generation. Always immaculately dressed and with a slightly swaggering walk, he was a very nice man in every way and an excellent and courageous driver of Bugatti, Maserati and ERA cars. His road cars consisted of a twelve cylinder Lagonda, an MG Magna Continental Coupe, a Type 57SC Bugatti two-seater fixed head coupe and several of the then new tiny Fiat 500's, all in his colour scheme of dark blue and black and without even having met him, Fred decided that Howe wouldn't like him — so he didn't like Howe.

Howe, known to everyone as 'The Old Man' was a popular president and was friendly to everyone, including motorcycle people. From time to time on practice days, he would take a stroll round the paddock greeting and chatting to people including myself. His opening gambit was always the same, a breezy "Morning — and how's Mortimer today" to which one felt bound to reply "Very well thank you Sir, how are you". Then, "Fine, fine thanks" after which there might or might not be more conversation depending on how many people were around. Talking to Howe was always interesting. One knew what cars he had been driving and in what races, and to some extent he knew ours. He enjoyed comparing Brooklands bike technique to cars and could never understand how it was possible to lap the track at over a hundred miles an hour on a bike using only the flat bottom bit of the Byfleet banking. I once recall asking him how many Fiat 500's he had — at the time I had my first one. "Fiat 500's? Lord, I don't know, Quite a few. Nice little blighters — wear 'em like my suits".

On the occasion of the Howe-Dixon dialogue, Fred was in trouble with the Riley and was laying on his back beneath the car. Recognising not only the car but also the protruding legs, Howe, perhaps not too tactfully, breezed up. "Morning — and how's Dixon today?" No immediate response but Fred slowly emerged and sat looking up — "Awreet — 'Ows 'Owe?" The 'Old Man' loved it and told the story to friends many times. Later that day there was an almost better sequel when, in the crowded Club Bar, Fred was being chided for rudeness by his friends, for just as there was a lull in the conversation, his voice rang out "I'm not being talked down to by any Bloody Duke" with, unknown to him, Howe just behind

him. The 'Old Man' handled it perfectly, moving with his small group further down the bar and when the next lull came, calling loudly "Dixon — Have a drink with a 'Bloody Duke'." From then on they became real friends, both on Christian name terms, 'Fred' and 'Francis'.

Among the nicer cars I bought and sold were a 4½ litre 100mph Low Chassis Invicta, a sparkling Auburn two-seater Speedster with outside chrome exhausts sprouting from its bonnet; a Cord; a Mercedes 36/220hp Foursome Coupe bodied by Corsica, and several Railtons. I loved and still love the Low Chassis Invicta and enjoyed driving all the others. The Cord took longest to sell and I didn't make the mistake of buying another. All the Railtons came from Thompson and Taylor who were Concessionaires and, by then, had showrooms in the paddock; all were 'trade-ins' and I would later be associated with their maker, Capt. Noel Macklin.

Though the E.F. JAP took me just about satisfactorily and once rather spectacularly through my first Brooklands racing season, always a crowd puller in view of its belt drive, it could only be run in handicap races in view of its age and small capacity, always receiving massive starts from the rest of the field. I didn't win a race with it but did notch up one or two 'seconds' and 'thirds'. Did I say 'spectacularly'? Well, yes, an amazing thing happened. The big star of those days was Ben Bickell who rode big and fast bikes. Ben, whom I knew well, was leading for the Outer Circuit Aggregate Award at the time, was looking for rides and after having the bike for a few days at his garage, rode it in a three lap handicap, doing some work on the engine and using his own 'nitro' fuel. Till then, the best lap I'd done, flat out all the way round, was a mere 58mph which was more or less in line with the Villiers engined one seven fives which were only slightly faster. Ben's ride ended on Lap Three with a rather big bang after a 'glittering' 59mph standing lap and a 'flyer' at 65mph. I still recall his brother Joe's remark when on removing the cambox cover, a broken cam follower fell out: "You poor little bleeder — not your fault — you were never designed to follow cams at those revs!" And again 'spectacular'. At a later meeting it caught fire on the start line and I still recall the callous spectators shouting from behind the railings: "Don't put it out. Let the poor little blighter burn!"

Though later, and with much better machinery, I became more successful, I was never dedicated to the point at which racing was the only thing in my life. I enjoyed dealing and, even more, the company of attractive young ladies. Girls, in those days were far less pretty than they are now and when my Radley school friend Johnny Waite told me about his latest, "the most beautiful you've ever seen Charles", I looked forward to meeting her and when I did I could only agree. Strelsa was tall, raven haired, articulate and on the stage in a big musical show on at the London Casino. At first we used to go on pub crawls as a threesome, and despite my friendship with Johnny, I just had to make progress. For a time she went out with one or the other of us but I felt that if real progress was to be made I must invest in a more suitable car for collecting at West End stage doors and hence, while I still retained my faithful Austin, I bought a low mileage SS1 Fixed Head Coupe, all bonnet with not much power under it from its two litre Standard engine. But it looked the part and helped to do the trick and led to many happy weekends when on Saturday nights I collected my 'goddess' from the Casino stage door en route for her parents' lovely house at Bognor.

The sidecar outings that year fell into the category of 'duty' runs, taking a different passenger each time, all chaps who had given help during the season and longed to know what the track was like. Johnny Waite, for instance, had given me endless help and it was with him on board that I threw away our best chance of the year, the Hutchinson '100', then a flat-out blind for 100 miles for solos, sidecars and three wheelers, on handicap. It looked good right from the start. Our handicap speed was certainly below what we knew we could do but, in the end, we 'blew it'. We were concerned only with E.G. Bishop who rode a 350cc Excelsior with sidecar and who, at the time, held the 350cc Sidecar lap record. We were both handicapped to start together and though he was faster, we hoped to be able to slipstream him at least till half distance when we came in to refill. But when the flag dropped, the Excelsior oiled a plug and he was only leaving the line when we came round for the first time. We came under the Members Bridge and off the Home banking together and did, in fact, manage to 'tuck in' behind him all the way till the refill. What happened then was awful.

Numerous supporters, finding us miles ahead on handicap, thronged our pit excitedly causing our own poorly rehearsed pit stop to be far worse than it would have been had our two rather inexpert pit attendants had the pit to themselves. All that had to be done was for two gallons of fuel to go in from a can (no quick fillers in those days!) and the oil tank to be topped up carefully, making sure that only what oil was needed went in. I truly think that that fill must have been the worst in the history of motor cycle racing at Brooklands. So many helpers getting in each others way and muttered appeals such as "Here, let me do it", "quick, give us a bit of rag", gave an idea as to what was going on. It was dreadful and cost us the race because despite it all we finished a close fifth at the end. A quick look down at the machine as we accelerated away up the hill from the pit and onto the Home banking was revealing, the engine glittering with spilt oil mixing with alcohol fuel streaming down the tank sides from over-filling. I recall thinking how lucky it wasn't petrol or that no one among the throng had apparently been smoking. It certainly was rather different in those days!

I continued to buy and sell, striking up an excellent business arrangement with 'Dunlop Mac'. From the racing point of view we were — correctly — rated as 'amateur' buying at reduced prices tyres we needed. This didn't amount to much since most of our races were short anyway. From time to time I used to visit 'The Chalet' for coffee and biscuits with 'Mac' and his team, discovering one day a mountain of half-used car and motor cycle racing tyres all part worn while some were hardly worn at all. Keenly interested I asked 'Mac' what they were. The answer was that almost all the 'big' car people, getting their tyres free, never started a long race without renewing them — and nor did the motorcycle profes-sionals. Many were motorcycle sizes discarded before professionals departed for the Isle of Man T.T. or other Grand Prix — and the pile was huge!

Were these covers available? He'd never thought about it, but could see no reason why not, though he wouldn't like to take money for them. On what basis could we trade? Well, Mac had a flutter with the bookmakers from time to time but hadn't the time to spend by the trackside with a watch as I did — maybe we could come to a barter arrangement which would be helped if I felt sure of winning a particular race myself. I was just glad that our talk hadn't taken place before the previous year's Hutchinson '100'! From then on I never recall buying a new racing tyre and years later when I was racing my Type 35B 2.3 Litre Bugatti I recall having to dig deep into the Dunlop pile and in the end finding some. When I showed them to Mac he called 'Fiddle'. "How long d'you reckon those

have been there?'' 'Fiddle' furrowed his brow. ''The last time I recall fitting those was when Howe had his Type 51.'' Thus I became a dealer in used racing tyres as well as everything else.

There was never a time when I had nothing to do. Thanks to the faithful Austin I collected urgently needed spares from anywhere, no matter how far away. Euston, St. Pancras, the Midlands or even further afield, my services were always in demand. Some racing cars belonging to wealthy owners were kept in 'one car' garages at the track where the owner's personal mechanic worked full time on them. From time to time cars would arrive back 'bent' after a race, with another race to follow next weekend. Time was then of the essence. I would help to strip and, if necessary set off in the Austin to get parts that were needed and later, when I was racing cars myself I sometimes was asked to test, out on the track. And under this heading there were often jobs which one man working alone couldn't handle. Really it was a 'spiv's' life but never the same each day, in a unique environment and a unique community. Never dull or repetitive, always rewarding and sometimes, very!

Years later I was reminded of it all by a conversation I heard in a Turkish bath in London between a quite well-known jockey and a car dealer who used to go when discussing business together. I got to know both quite well and found that the jockey was a car enthusiast whose opinion on cars was often valued by the owners of the horses he rode, the result of which was that, from time to time, they bought cars from him, supplied by his car dealer friend at prices way below those they would have had to pay in a big showroom. This time they were having one of their famous rows — which everyone there enjoyed. The car dealer called the jockey ''A clapped out nag pilot'' and got the reply ''So that's what I

The first of a long series of Speed Six Bentleys. This one has coachwork by Freestone & Webb.

am. Right mate I'll tell you what I do. Half the time when I'm not riding, I spend my time living like a gentleman, feeding in the best restaurants and living in the best hotels. And what am I doing when I'm working? I'll tell you. Riding the best meat in the world, mixing with the nobility and gentry and squiring their daughters.'' It all went down well and needless to say, both were Cockneys — and the best of friends, still dealing happily together next time I saw them. By the end of 1933 I still had the Austin but the SS1 had been replaced by a 'Speed Six' Bentley 6½ litre, registered PG6345, with an even longer bonnet and much more performance than the SS, and with a Foursome Coupe Body by Freeston & Webb, more prestigious, faster from London to Bognor but, even then, not at its best in town.

I spotted PG6345 outside a Hammersmith pub one morning thinking what a wonderful 'White Elephant' it was and how well it would fit in with all the others I'd bought at Aldridges. So into the pub I went, finding only one other customer there, who turned out to be the owner. Nearly everyone who was using a big car at that time wanted to

sell it and Mr. Edgar fitted into the pattern in that respect so that was the first of a series of 'Speed Sixes' for me. That must have been around the time I first met Charles Brackenbury who, even then, was well established as a successful driver of Bugattis at Brooklands. Later on Charles, a versatile driver if ever there was one, drove many other cars of all sizes from John Cobb's Napier Railton, in record attempts, John's ex Campbell Sunbeam 12 Cyl 'Tiger' in the B.R.D.C. 500 Miles Race, six and twelve cylinder Lagondas, and Aston Martins at Le Mans and numerous others. His life really revolved round Brooklands and he and George Harvey Noble who later held the 750cc Brooklands outer circuit record at over 118mph always came to the bike meetings to act as track marshals after which there was a party which started in the clubhouse and, more often than not, would finish in London. Either would enliven any party and one never knew what might happen in their company.

Later on when I had come to an arrangement with Robin Jackson to drive his 1½ litre single seater Alta in sprints, I remember an absolutely dreadful day we spent together en route for the Lewes Speed Trials. Charles had heard about it and announced that he would take me down but I tried to get out of it because Robin was keen that the car should do well and, knowing Charles, one felt that at best we would be late and might not even get there. But he insisted and in the end I lost. Knowing him, I made the point that we must start early, secretly hoping that, with luck, we might arrive before the pubs opened. Approaching Brighton he announced that he wanted to call at an antique shop and this surprised me because I'd no idea that he was interested in antiques or even knew anything about them. The 'antique' shop turned out not be an antique shop at all but just an almost derelict shop filled with junk, kept by an old man wearing a long leather coat who, when he saw Charles uttered the one word "No", from which I assumed that he'd either been there before, on his own or with George. Charles looked surprised.

"What d'you mean — 'No'?" "I mean 'no' — not again, after last time. I'm not having you in here." "Why not? I've come miles to do business with you." "What business?" "Well, that coat for a start. I'd like to buy it." "It's not for sale. Go on now. Clear off." "Well those chairs, then," pointing to eight chairs which weren't really chairs at all and would have found better use as firewood. But he bought them and paid some little boys to take them down to the seafront saying that the council hadn't provided enough seats there. He went on to buy a dreadful stuffed Golden pheasant in a cage and an upright piano with no strings, arranging to have the latter consigned to poor Bill Cotton, who was then playing at the Palladium with his 'Billy Cotton Band Show' before leaving with the pheasant and cage, well wrapped.

"Tell you what. We'll have an early lunch at the Bodega. There'll be nothing laid on at Lewes." So to the Bodega we went . The

first words of the Manager, Mr. Fuller, were "Look Charles. Nice to see you and your friends. But be a good chap — no nonsense", as he led us to a remote corner, leaving us with a menu. "I'll send the waiter to you." The rest of the story doesn't need telling. The Bodega hadn't got pheasant on the menu so, after unwrapping his purchase, breaking open the cage and disappearing with 'his' pheasant he made his way to the kitchen with it. A hubbub in the kitchen and he returned with it on a large metal tray, feathers blazing, acrid smoke trail astern to sit down and grasp a carving knife to the waiter's horror and Mr. Fuller's wrath.

But we did get to Lewes in time and the rest of the day went well. Even the Alta, which had a reputation for temperament, won the 1½ litre Racing car class, coming second in the 2 litre and fourth in the Unlimited.

A rather comic correspondence arose in the motoring press later because since, in the 1½ litre class run, the car broke the course record, we used this to advertise my business down in Byfleet whereupon Peter Monkhouse whose ERA had come second, wrote in pointing out that his car had put up a faster time in its 2 litre run and that he should therefore be the 1500cc record holder. But the official answer to that was no: since his faster run was done in the bigger capacity class, our time in the 1½ litre must stand as the record. All good fun and had I been in his position, I would have felt the same. Our run home that day involved many stops for refreshment and couldn't have been safely done today.

That was one side of Charles. But in all the time I knew him, I never recall seeing him in a bar prior to a big race and, on race days, only after the race itself. He was a very versatile, courageous and skilled driver, determined and dependable.

PG6345 remains a memory for two reasons, the first being that it was the first car I owned fitted with a radio and the second for something awful that it did to me on a run from Weybridge to the Norton factory in Birmingham. Like all of its kind, it was at its best on a long, straight road, seldom being challenged by other makes or types. But as time went on it was sometimes hard pressed by the later 3½ litre Jaguars or 4½ Bentleys and it was on one of these occasions that it gave me a fright. It happened somewhere between Oxford and Birmingham where, after being pressed on a twisty road section, we came to a long straight which ended with a fast lefthand bend. The straight helped to hold off the 4½ but as we went into the bend, the steering seemed heavy and there was a rather strange sort of noise. Suddenly, with almost no warning and with all the weight of the car on it, the offside front wheel collapsed, locking the steering completely. Fortunately there was nothing coming the other way or it would have been disastrous. But one couldn't really blame it, for despite its pristine appearance, it was an old car even then. Sorry as I was to see it go, it was and always felt a very big car, thirsty fuelwise and always a problem

to park even then. By the time it departed, I didn't want another Speed Six though later I had three others.

Its replacement was a circa 1929 Chrysler fabric-bodied foursome coupe, not as fast but a good and more refined and usable car but its artillery type wheels appeared rather dated even then. But it was reliable, trouble free and quite fun to drive and had nothing like the thirst of the Bentley. Again, I don't recall its departure but its successor was another SS1 Foursome Coupe, the later type with rather shorter bonnet but a full four seater. It's ownership was short for, good value as the early SS models were, they always felt like a souped up Standard to drive.

There'd been many races in 1933 and 1934 and far too few successes. There was a saying among both car and bike people that if one wanted to win races then race a slow machine but if one wanted fun, race a fast one. I wanted both so settled for one of the new unit-construction, 150cc New Imperials and the 1000cc Brough Superior and the saying proved to be true. The New Imperial was new, supplied by our local agent, Henry

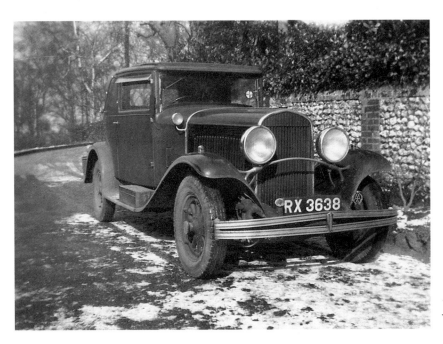

1929 Chrysler Coupe. A good reliable car. Not so fast as the Bentley, but not so thirsty either.

Nash, the Brough much older and, initially a pig to ride.

With such a wide variety of machinery competing at Brooklands at the time, individual handicapping was really the only way to run the event and the standard of handicapping was, on the whole, excellent. Outer circuit races always started at the Fork, by the big Vickers Shed. With the Brough one was usually near the shed end of the start line on or near the Scratch mark. The starter would first flag off the slowest machines, one seven fives and two fifties, working his way towards the scratch mark via the three fifties, five hundreds with sidecars, seven fifties and then the fastest machines. If on the scratch mark the wait seemed interminable, the limit men sometimes coming through at the end of their first lap in a three lap race before one got the flag so that, in three laps, they had to be passed twice. With a slow machine from the 'limit' mark one got the flag first and might not see a single machine or rider throughout the race until, while thinking that this really was going to be a win, one was swamped by half a dozen faster runners, — all rather dull and frustrating! It would be nice to be able to say that, conversely, with the Brough, one got a great grandstand view of the race but it wasn't that way at all, — life was far too exciting!

Its maximum was circa 110mph so a 'Gold Star' lap should have been a cakewalk. It was the reverse because, when delivery was taken, an essential damper had been removed from the front fork assembly: with that replaced, it was transformed. But years later when riding five hundreds, it was astonishing to find how much easier a three figure lap was. Even then, tyres were a problem so that one had to take a 'thousand' round on the 'top line' of the bankings just ten feet below the top. The reverse applied with a five hundred: ten feet from the inside edge, where it was unbanked, was the norm, and

the bike would go round the Byfleet side in a 100mph plus slide for the whole three quarter mile distance. Though the 150cc and 1000cc duo did work, it was anything but ideal. The 'tiddler' certainly won races on handicap but was tiresomely tedious to ride. In contrast, the Brough only won one.

But the snag was that there were too few races in which to run either, the B.M.C.R.C's policy at that time being to go for eight race programmes, the first four on the Outer circuit and the others 'Round the Mountain' so, with a road racing set up one could run on both circuits at the same meeting and this, more than anything else contributed to a change to Nortons in 1935.

For a mere £25, the Brough was good value and had served its purpose and, in a way, gave a stupid feeling of superiority for, later, when one heard riders of smaller capacity machines complaining of handling problems on the Outer Circuit , one could counter with "You think you've got problems — try it on a 'Thousand'." The fact that, at the time, only about one big twin was regularly running at the track to twenty or more 'singles' proved the point. So both bikes went, the Brough sold outright and the little 'one fifty' New Imperial part exchanged for a two fifty 'Grand Prix' model of the same make which broke cam followers more and more regularly the faster one made it go, punctured its rear tyre half way through the 'Hutchinson' hundred mile race but did manage to finish third in the 100 Mile Brooklands Grand Prix.

The Chrysler departed at the end of that year, with quite a lot of regret because it had been completely trouble free and a consistently good performer. I think the reason was that at the time, I was low in stock, needed money and hadn't enough in hand to pay its road fund tax. That was the first time I'd found myself needing both saleable stock and money at the same time — but over the years it was not the last. Luckily, it was late in the season so, from then until the following spring I really got down to work to get matters sorted out. Looking back for the cause of it all, I had to admit that 'women' were behind it — I liked the attractive ones and, even then, they didn't come cheaply. Fortunately, I had no thoughts at all of marriage at the time!

One thing that deterred me was a speech made by a famous, much married, rider, the Guest of Honour at our local motorcycle club and much admired and envied by us all. In it he said that he was sorry to hear that so many members of the club were getting married because he'd decided that nothing slowed a man's racing career more than marriage, except possibly a serious racing accident — and in many ways the two things were very similar!

I remained a member of that club for years, the Leatherhead and District, and in fact rode my very first race — and won it — at one of their grass track meetings and Randalls Park way back in 1932. The machine was unique and very attractive — an AETC. You've never heard of it — I'm not surprised. It was a work project of the Automobile Engineering Training College,

designed by one group of students and constructed by others, and I believe almost everything except wheels, tyres and saddle were made within the works. It was for several years a showpiece, mounted on a dais in the entrance hall, later relegated to an outbuilding till I asked whether I could buy it, and did so.

The AETC had a 175cc two stroke engine and I still recall vividly its first and last great race. It teemed with rain as I pushed it from Dorking to Leatherhead, a twenty mile return trip. The 'speedway' at Randall's Park was in a field on a hill so that the lower part became a morass of mud even after the morning practice sessions — and it teemed all day. The 175cc race was the first of the day and brought forth just three starters, one of whom fell off at the start, the second becoming stuck at the bottom so it was not too hard a race to win. I also remember finding that the first prize was a 'Silver Cup' and that, not receiving it, I wrote to the Secretary asking why. Later, it came by post direct from the supplier, not silver, four inches high, engraved and bearing its price tag — Two Shillings and Sixpence!

Surprising Successes

Looking back, at the end of 1934, on my first three years spent at Brooklands, the sum total seemed to have been many laughs, a lot of fun, a few wins and odd seconds & thirds and a 1000cc Gold Star. But I could see that the two big mistakes I'd made were, first, in racing without a goal or any policy and second in making too many changes of machine. It was interesting to see that when I had started to have a policy at the beginning of 1934, it had produced a few results. So for 1935 I made a policy and resolved to stick to it. The plan was to get a new 500cc Manx Norton and, if possible, a Manx 350cc as well and to do road racing events as well as Brooklands Outer Circuit races. There were two snags the cost and, also that never having ridden on the road, I had no idea whether or not, I could go fast round corners! Both became resolved before the 1935 Season started.

1935 turned out to be a very good year. For transport I had a really great 36/220hp Mercedes Sports Foursome Coupe. I had had one earlier among my 'For Sale' stock which had turned out to to be rather a pig but UL5100 turned out to be cast in a different mould. The strange thing was that while looking rather evil and menacing, with her flared wings and huge outside exhausts, she really was a perfect lady. Together we covered more mileage that year than in any other car I'd owned except the Austin, one of the fastest and best journeys being a very early morning one from Dorking to Norwich in glorious weather, the object being to try and buy yet another 36/220, this time a sports four-seater tourer. The vendor turned

A very pretty Mercedes 36/220 with coachwork by Corsica. One of the many attractive sports cars owned by the author during the 1930s.

out to be a nice man, who after the deal was done, insisted on take me out to lunch, 'lunch' consisting of one of the most mammoth pub crawls imaginable. The purchase of that car had a rather testing sequel also because it was with Brackenbury that I went in the open car to see Shelsley for the first time, a week or two later.

All had gone as well as could be expected on a trip with Charles till just after leaving Shelsley we came across a trio of itinerant musicians 'thumbing' a lift back to London, one armed with a trumpet, another with a clarinet and the third with a trombone, not at all an uncommon sight in the 1930's. Would we give them a lift in the right direction, they asked. This was obviously right up Charles' street. Yes we would, he said, but on one condition, that they played their instruments all the way home. A short conference between them and, almost enthusiastically, they agreed, for even if they failed, they would get part of the way. And for the best part of an hour they kept it up, much to the astonishment of the Worcester-shire and Wiltshire inhabitants as we passed through their countryside. And when at last they retired breathless, the condition was eased so that we took them most of the way on the basis of their playing through the towns only. It must have been quite a sight, a huge Mercedes with orchestral accompani-ment!

The big Manx Norton of 1935 was a super bike, not too fast as one received it from the works but responsive to basic tuning, reliable and easy to work on. Its handling was at least as good as any other make and better than most and so were its brakes. I took the Austin with its trailer to collect mine early in February from the Bracebridge Street factory in Birmingham and had it out for its first Brooklands practice run a few weeks later. It came, as ordered, with a Brooklands silencer already fitted and running on a 50/50 Petrol Benzole mixture.

There was paper work with it including a graph showing the power curve on the Brake Test; it required no running in and, on that first outing lapped at just over ninety five — not fast enough to be really competi-tive but it was the way that it handled that gave such confidence and hope, and I longed to be able to acquire a three fifty as a stablemate. It began to win races for me right from the start, the first big one being the Mountain Circuit Wakefield Trophy race at the B.M.C.R. Cup Day Meeting where it won, first its heat and then the final.

One just couldn't put a foot wrong with it and even if one did, it was so forgiving that it got one out of trouble almost before it started. It won and was placed in a number of other less important Brooklands races and then was entered for the 500cc Mountain Championship, a 25 lap Scratch race on the 'Mountain' circuit. This was always very much of a 'tear-up' with all the best riders and machinery competing, people like Harold Daniell and all the Cambridge crowd including Jock Forbes and others so that normally one would have been content with any place down to tenth. The 'Tear-up' became fact and with it a big mortality rate, partly from machinery but also with leaders finishing 'on the floor' so that, amazingly, the Norton and I found ourselves 'Cham-pions', both of us knowing that we were really nothing of the sort but just fairly good supporting players aided by the disasters of others. Even so, it was encouraging, and 1935 was like that all the way through. Or nearly all the way!

The Brooklands 100 Mile Grand Prix, a month or two later, was a day of mixed fortune. It was generally accepted that Harold Daniell would emerge winner of the Senior (500cc) 100 mile Grand Prix and Les Archer the Junior (350cc) and, by then, I had added a three fifty Norton and had entered both races. Les was partnered by Neil Christmas, also Velocette mounted, and the

One of author's Manx Nortons pictured in the lay-by on the Byfleet Banking, from where they did most of their testing and development.

big threat to the Velocettes came from two works AJS to be ridden by George Rowley and Reg Barber. My three fifty, for all it's good looks, turned out to be resistant to its Brooklands silencer and was well down on speed but, following its win in the Mountain Championship, its big sister was right on song. But two days before the races the Velocette firm, wanting to be sure of victory in the Junior, came up with two works three fiftys for Les and Neil; Les, knowing my 'three fifty' problems, offered me his own machine. There were only slight strings attached. He had felt sure of winning on his own bike so it was essential that Velocettes now finished first, second and third. We tried all three bikes together on the outer circuit and the one I was to ride lapped at

ninety four compared to the works machines' ninety seven and, on the day we did finish 1-2-3 with Les and Neil a long way ahead and mine next just one second ahead of George's AJS.

For me it was rather a tense race, often with one AJS ahead and the other a yard or two astern and, once or twice, with one on each side. The Velocette was great, but it didn't fit me and, at the end, I was so 'knackered' that the five hundred ride at first seemed daunting. The day was hot and I was thirsty. At that time I was a beer drinker but well meaning friends prescribed 'Scotch'; though, till then, I'd never tried it, I sunk what I was given and made for the start blissfully unaware that I'd just sunk a 'treble' in record time. No pre-race nerves on the line as usual — just a sensation of confidence and optimism: I should have known better! The flag fell. The machine just felt a bit heavier than usual to push but it fired instantly — and we were away with some jostling as we turned left at the end of the finishing straight onto the outer and down the Railway Straight to 'the Byfleet'. Surprisingly, I saw I was lying fourth, about six or eight places higher than expected in a race of that length and quality. Only Nortons seemed to be ahead and for two or three laps it stayed that way. Then it all seemed rather boring and I decided to 'have a go' at the third man, Tony Rawlence and without even waiting one more lap to decide where and

how, I dived close in and passed actually in the Finishing straight chicane. Coming out, adhesion at the front end disappeared and, for the first time, I was 'on the floor' with the machine still rattling along on its side and 'end over end' which clearly spelt the end. It was some time before I tried 'Scotch' again.

We knew at this time that something was brewing at Eric Fernihough's garage down on the Brooklands Road and when the 'something' turned out to be the building of a Brough Superior 'thousand' in conjunction with George Brough himself with the object of breaking, first, the Brooklands bike lap record and, later, the World Land Speed

Hereby hangs a tale. Having finished 3rd in the 350cc Brooklands Grand Prix the author took a couple of swift whiskies before the 500cc class. For one reason or another his handlebar hit the barrel on the right and Charles landed in a sitting position. A fellow competitor gives him a cheery thumbs up sign.

record, we became very interested despite all the security and secrecy. To try to penetrate the screen, I stopped there as often as possible for petrol and while filling one evening a van arrived delivering a large size Brooklands racing sidecar. Why, one wondered, and then it dawned. Noel Pope was then lap record holder, the first to lap the track at over 120mph and Henne, BMW-mounted, held the Land Speed Record at circa 170mph. Despite his expertise on 175's, 250's and 350's Eric had never ridden a machine of higher capacity at the track, though he did have an almost unbeatable '500' for sprints. So the sidecar was for the Brough, to slow down the speed a bit while doing initial tests. Would he be taking ballast or a passenger — if the latter, then I would like the job.

Next day he was up in the canteen so, joining him, I said quietly, "By the way, Eric, if you're taking a passenger in the sidecar of the Brough, I'd like to apply for the job". He looked flabbergasted. "What are you talking about?" "Well, it's a very big sidecar — far too big for a five hundred, and you don't like sidecars anyway. You've been working here for weeks behind locked doors so obviously you're up to something. Taking it a stage further, you're going to fit that sidecar to whatever it is you're building — which can only be a 'Thousand', probably a Brough because nobody else but George would want to give support. So why a sidecar? Because the bloody thing's going to be so fast that you want added weight to slow it down for initial testing. After that — the Outer Circuit record for a start, some sprints maybe, and an odd race or two and then who knows?''

I put the last bit in because I thought he just might have his eye on the bike World Land Speed Record — which, of course he had. So I saw the Brough Superior for the first time and did passenger him in the 'chair' every time he used it. Every trip seemed

more electrifying than the last. We did about a dozen tests at the track over a period of about a month, many of which were standing start half miles, working out on the Railway Straight. To do a standing start, the power was so great that one couldn't just "point it and gun it". It had to be pointed not in the direction one planned to go but at forty five degrees to the right, so that when one dropped the clutch one did so on full right lock, correcting gradually as the bike tried its best to run round the side car. It really was quite an experience and after all, it was almost certainly the fastest bike in the world at that time, with a maximum speed solo of over 170mph and with sidecar circa 140mph.

Its first competitive outing was at a very small sprint meeting which seemed rather a strange choice but wasn't for two reasons, the first being that he wanted the smallest audience possible and the second being that the meeting was run by the Cambridge University Club, the University to which Eric had been. Doing it that way he couldn't be accused of 'pot hunting' and his Cambridge friends would be the first to see the outfit in operation. Needless to say it won both sidecar and solo classes and made mincemeat of both records. Held at Syston, it was a long and tiring day with a four o'clock morning start, Eric driving his early 'Bullnose Morris' type MG sports tourer, Francis Beart in attendance and myself in the back. It rained and the journey from Weybridge to Syston seemed interminable but we got there in the end to be welcomed by the committee — and George Brough himself. The bike and sidecar, the latter loaded with tools and spares, followed behind the car on a self steering attachment and, strangely, it didn't seem so far on the way home.

Next outing, was the Brighton Speed Trials — along the seafront. First in both Classes, easily, and both course records shattered. And on it went — first the Brooklands

Outer Circuit from Noel Pope's Brough at 123mph. And later came the World Record attempt which ended in disaster.

But quite a lot was to happen before that because there was paddock talk among the bike people about going to have a 'go' in a

The author's friend Eric Fernihough with the Brough Superior on which he was killed whilst attempting to beat the 170mph Land Speed Record.

Eric Fernihough and the 2 litre Riley with which he had intended to take up car racing. Sadly this was not to be.

Continental road race and, in the end, a party was made up consisting of Francis Beart with my old two fifty New Imperial, Neil Christmas with his Velocette 'Three Fifty' and Tony Rawlence and myself with five hundred Nortons. It all came about rather strangely. Eric did quite a number of Continental races with his 175cc and 250cc bikes and since the smaller capacity classes were less hotly contested, he made money at it.

Neil, Tony, Francis and I were all in our early twenties at that time and, by comparison with Eric who was older, we were sometimes rather wild, particularly if led by Noel Pope who had held the outer circuit lap record until Eric took it. Our fun was usually noisy but harmless but we knew that Eric disapproved. On this occasion we had read in one of the journals that he was going to compete in the Dieppe Grand Prix so, without telling him, we sent for Regulations, requested appearance money from the organisers, got it, if modestly, and put in our entries. Though today it seems strange, we had none of us been abroad or spoke much French, and when Eric got wind of it he was horrified and came along and read us the riot act, the gist of it being that we mustn't behave in France as we did at Brooklands. In retrospect he was right and what worried him was that his reputation as a professional stood high abroad and he didn't want it ruined.

We were all short of money, as most people were at that time, for the big recession of the early 1930's was still being felt in England — so the trip had to be done cheaply, transporting the machines from Brooklands to Newhaven, crossing by night (for cheapness!) and arriving at Dieppe in the very early hours and riding the bikes, unlit and on open exhausts, to the Hotel Maison Blanche which was on the course. I still recall our arrival in Dieppe, at two o'clock on a pitch black morning in drizzling rain.

Though always a good starter, my five hundred oiled a plug on the jetty and by the time I'd changed it the rest had gone so, appalled by the noise, I pottered through the town and somehow got onto the right road for the three mile ride to the hotel. I could hardly believe the sight that met me. Had it been an English pub, everyone would have been waiting outside trying to waken someone for admission. But, no, there it was, the restaurant brilliantly lit and the whole gang tucking into coffee and bacon and eggs and croissants. My first sight of France and it has never changed. At six o'clock we were out on the course for the first practice. A long uphill straight came first, then right onto a shorter one, into a small village, turn right into a dung-strewn main street and a long twisty climbing section, tree-lined, back to the right hand hairpin at the Maison Blanche.

It really was a fabulous weekend because, our races apart, the main event was the Car Grand Prix with all the best Continentals, such as Chiron, Dreyfus, Wimille and Benoist driving Monoposto Alfas and Bugatti Type 59s after we had raced as 'warmers up' for the crowds. And we not only did well, we won what was, to us, a lot of money, Neil winning the three fifty class, Eric the 175cc while after a long battle with Cora's works Sarolea, I came second in the 500cc. The highlight of it all was the prizegiving at the Casino, to which we had to go to collect our winnings. Arriving slightly late through having to walk there, we were routed through the kitchens, just astern of Freddie Dixon and Charles Brackenbury, also late. The cabaret was about to go on, consisting of a huge, stripped to the waist, turbanned chap, about to carry in a pretty girl sitting on a large brass tray. The girl was sitting cross-legged on the kitchen table and this was altogether too much for Fred. Picking up the tray and balancing it and the protesting young lady he marched on to the stage to what really was tumultuous applause from

Charles Mortimer (number 58) at the Maison Blanc in the 1935 Senior Dieppe Grand Prix. Not much in the way of crowd control — or crowd!

all. It was a very good evening with the 'pièce de resistance' being transported back to the hotel in a Bugatti Type 49. Certainly a weekend to be remembered!

Returning on the boat the next day I had thoughts about what the future aims should be. I was now a Brooklands Gold Star holder in the 1000cc and 500cc classes and wanted to make it a triple with a 100mph lap with a three fifty, and wanted, somehow, to be a holder of World Records, even if they didn't stand for long. Even in 1935 World War Two seemed to be inevitably coming closer and there might not be much time in which to 'have a go' with cars and, in that sphere, I wanted to, at least, win a race or two and get a car Star for a lap at over 120mph. The problem with record breaking was that all the short distance World Records, say from the Mile to 100 Miles, were held by works machinery specially constructed for the task. One had to think in terms of a long, long ride with correspondingly high track and timekeeper's fees and quite a high risk of the machinery failing at some stage. So I talked to Eric Fernihough

about this one and a few days later he came up with the answer, which was that it could be done at Brooklands and that if I would underwrite the track and timekeepers fees in the event of failure, he would provide, prepare and maintain a machine in the 250cc Class, arrange all bonus payments from accessory manufacturers, and partner an attempt on all World Records from the Six Hours to 12 Hours, to be attempted in October, the month available in which he had no Continental race commitments.

October wasn't an ideal month, weather apart, because starting the run at eight o'clock in the morning, stopping eight times to refuel and and change riders, and with no possibility of getting even one record till we'd been running for six hours, there would still be the problem of the last two hours being done in darkness and with no lights. I asked him who would ride out first and he said he'd like to, so as to be sure the bike was alright; I worked out the roster and found that, on that basis, while he'd be having only about half an hour of riding at the end of the day, I'd have an hour and a half, to which he replied "I don't think it will be necesssary. If the thing breaks, it'll break long before that. If not I reckon we'll have broken the 12 Hour record by ten hours".

So we did it, with a superbly prepared 250cc Cotton, breaking every World Record from Six to 12 Hours, including the Mile and Kilo ones, twelve in all. Eric had recently had an appendicitis operation and when, at six o'clock that evening, we were two hours in hand, he refused to go on. I wanted to build up as big a margin as possible once we'd got that far, so set off again in the dark. Being October it was very dark and thousands of rabbits on the track made it worse because one kept hitting them. The front of the machine was a mass of blood and fur when I came in at seven, really having had enough, but George Reynolds, the most kind and helpful of the timekeepers was urging me to go on, saying that we could cut the speed down and run in the headlights of Eric's Railton, provided the back wheel of the bike was ahead of the front of the car. So that's what we did, covering between eight and nine hundred miles in the end, the machine's maximum being just over 90mph. Measuring the engine capacity afterwards became a bit of a panto-mime. George agreed the stroke immediately but spent some minutes measuring the bore. Then, standing up he wearily said "Very interesting. We started with a capacity of 246cc. Now I make it 244cc. The reason for that is that the cylinder has gone slightly oval and has contracted one way more than it's worn the other. But it's certainly under 250cc".

Eric stayed in bed the whole of the next day and didn't surface till mid morning. We had both thought our legs were aching during the night but, in daylight it turned out to be bruising. Next morning we had a

Riding this 250 Cotton at Brooklands in 1935 the author and Eric Fernihough broke every world class record from 6 to 12 hours. Financial rewards were not impressive, but they killed nearly 100 rabbits during the dark hours and Eric sold most of these to a local butcher.

financial reckoning. My share turned out to be £20 plus £2, being half the amount paid by the local butcher for rabbits killed and in marketable condition. I suggested to Eric that, as I had ridden through most of the darkness, I ought to have all the rabbit money but he said "No way. You don't have to clean the bloody thing. Have you seen the state it's in?" I let it go at that. The bike certainly was in a gory mess.

Nineteen Thirty Six was a good year from the racing point of view with a number of wins and many seconds and thirds and my first drive at Brooklands in a car. Both five hundred and three fifty Nortons were ready well in advance and I'd spent a week at the factory watching the engines built and tested on the brake so had learned a lot which, later, produced additional income. Many owners, mainly members of Clubs, wanted their bikes tuned and the most valuable thing I learned was the sensitivity of the overhead camshaft Norton engine to valve timing, particularly when running with a Brooklands silencer.

The timing was infinitely variable and could be altered without removing the engine from the frame by means of a Vernier adjustment in the cambox. The technique, which could produce an increase in lap speed of up to ten miles an hour, consisted of first recording the lap speed of the machine as received from its owner. Then stage by stage one made small adjustments to the valve timing via the Vernier, recording the lap speed after each change of timing until no change of timing produced better results in terms of lap speed.

The whole process could usually be completed in a morning though sometimes it might take slightly longer. Casting the word around, mainly via the motorcycle Clubs, that I was able to undertake 'tuning' of Norton engines produced a steady flow of customers, the charges being at the rate of £1 per mile an hour increase in lap speed.

But to add an atmosphere of 'mystique' to the thing, we used to specify the machine being left with us for a week. To ensure that the customer was getting value for his money we suggested, always, that he should bring a friend with him who, if he wished, could time the bike himself while the owner rode it while, of course, we timed it as well. We always preferred the owner to ride the first test himself because it was likely that, with little knowledge of Brooklands, he would probably be slower than a 'regular' who, on the final test could produce a mile or two an hour improvement on 'local' knowledge alone. The process was repeated on handing the bike back after completion of the work, always with one of us riding, even if the owner wanted to have another 'go' himself, the better of the two lap times counting regarding payment. With two or, sometimes, three bikes being 'doctored' per week, it was a golden era.

The highlights of 1936 were the winning of the Wakefield Trophy for the second year running, this time on the Outer Circuit and with the three fifty at 95.59mph, in May, a fourth in the Brooklands Senior 100 Mile Grand Prix in July and a win by the narrowest possible of margins in the 'Gold Star' race later in the season. This was an innovation, a two lap Outer Circuit race for Gold Star Holders alone, the highlight of it being entries from both Noel Pope and Eric Fernihough with their big Brough Superiors, Noel's earlier machine being supercharged.

The line up for the race was small with Eric on the Scratch mark conceding only two seconds start to Noel, six seconds to Tom Atkins' supercharged Douglas, eighteen seconds to 500cc Lap Record Holder Ben Bickell's Bickell-JAP and twenty seconds to Jock West on the works Triumph, Betty Shilling's Norton and myself. Betty Shilling was a qualified engineer as well as a Gold Star Holder, one of only three ladies, I think, to have lapped at over a hundred at the time.

On the line, no one felt that they were getting enough start from the two Broughs despite the fact that, with so short a race, their riders were likely to have problems of passing almost from the start. And to me it felt strange to be on the 'limit' end of the start line with a good five hundred capable of lapping at around a hundred and six. In the end, it was the old story: if you wanted to win handicap races at Brooklands, then ride a slow machine — if you wanted excitement, ride a fast one. I emerged winner at an average of 99.51mph with Eric second and Ben Bickell third. A dull race, really. I just put my head down, hung on, and never saw a soul. From Eric's point of view it was awful. He'd wanted to win the fastest bike race ever run at the track and had missed it by a hundredth of a second through being unable to find room to pass Noel at the very moment he needed it. Some idea of the acceleration of his Brough could be got by his standing lap of 102.69mph — only three miles an hour slower than my flying one. His 'Flyer' was 117.46 — probably eight miles an hour slower than he would have managed with a clear run.

Sadly, that was, I think, his last race. Keeping that machine, he went on to build another identical but supercharged one for an attack on the World's Motorcycle Speed Record. A semi-streamlined project which, after several successful preliminary runs, went out of control in the course of the attempt. He was a great loss to us all and his country.

That, and the fact that, only a few months later, Ben Bickell lost his life when racing in Ireland made me have thoughts I'd never had before regarding racing but, at the time, I told myself that Brooklands was far safer and that, anyway, I would soon be switching from bikes to cars. But even that illusion was also shattered within a month.

I was keen to have rather a strong 'go' in the Hutchinson 100 after making a hash of

the 1933 race with the Chater Lea and sidecar and retiring with a flat rear tyre on the two fifty New Imperial in 1934. I can't recall what I rode in 1935 — I think that was the one run in a downpour with saw me out with a magneto but no sparks. The 'Hutch' was always run in October and by then my five hundred was showing signs of tiredness so I decided to use the smaller one. To be sure of a trouble-free run, I asked J. S. (Woolley) Worters, a great manager and tuner, to do the engine for me provided he could have the complete machine so as to be sure that no other part failed and let his engine preparation down. A highly successful rider in his day and later a manager, 'Woolley' crowned his career by constructing Chris Staniland's Multi Union, the second fastest car ever to go round Brooklands. Expert as he was, he was a bit of a martinet and could, at times, be difficult, and though he lived quite near the track, he seldom went there at that stage of his life. But when I went to collect the machine, I saw that he'd swapped the usual Norton flat bed racing handlebars for an ubelievably narrow pair of low-set track racing type, the idea being to bring the riding position lower to reduce wind resistance. I was unhappy, particularly with their narrowness, right from the start but said nothing at the the time and refitted the originals once back at my shed in the paddock.

On the morning of the race, in strode 'Woolley', stopping dead in his tracks when he saw the bike. "What have you done that for?", he growled. I could see the hassle brewing. "They were too narrow. It's a hundred miles and I want to be comfortable." "Really!" He paused. "Well I can tell you this, Charles. If one of my riders had done that it would have been the finish for him. In terms of time what would you say the difference would be in lap times?". "Oh, a second per lap?". "Right. Thirty seven laps, thirty seven seconds. Races have been won by one tenth of that time.'' Turning on his heel he strode out.

The bike performed perfectly, finishing sixth at 94.50mph just ahead of Noel Pope's similar three fifty. Sure enough, there stood 'Woolley' still glowering. ''D'you know how far you were behind the second man?'' A stupid question because I was still sitting on the machine. ''No''. ''The I'll tell you. Sixteen seconds. Cost you second place.'' And he was right.

Two Wheels Good – Four Wheels Better

For some time past, I'd noticed a lovely little 750cc, supercharged MG pointed-tail 'Q' Type in Robin Jackson's place in the paddock and found out that he had it there for hire in short races. So I strode in boldly one day and asked if he'd hire it to me. To my amazement, he agreed at once. I asked the fee and when I could have it. "Well you can have it for the Whitsun Meeting if you want it. I've been charging £25 per race with a mechanic to look after it. But you don't want a mechanic, do you? You know enough about the track and don't need to know anything about the car. Practice with it and let me know if you've got any problems. On that basis, how about a fiver?"

A generous offer — but I felt I'd like to have a mechanic in case there were problems. "All right, then. £7. Practice with it early as you can on Saturday before we get busy so we can count on the mechanic for other problems later in the day. And you can have the chap all day on Monday. I'll put the entry in."

But when I arrived at nine o'clock the 'Robinery' had problems galore. Baker Carr's big single-seater Bentley was one of them and though the 'Q' type was ready, no mechanics were available. Robin came across. "Look, Charlie. We've enough problems at the moment to last us a lifetime. Take the car. Do what you like, and bring it back when you've finished". So I did.

No problems with starting — it even had a self starter. I hadn't admitted to not having used a pre-selector box recently but that was no problem either — and out I went, slowly up the hill at the end of the finishing straight, turning left at the end on to the outer circuit. As I turned, a red 2.3 Monza Alfa Romeo shot out from under the Members Bridge at between 125-130mph, very high on the banking, its driver apparently fighting a slide, still on full song, hitting the big bump awkwardly and landing almost sideways, finally crashing through the big fence between the track and the railway and demolishing it as it ploughed on, in a cloud of dust and debris.

Squirting the Midget hard, I parked it in the layby at the start of the Railway Straight and after waiting for a gap in the traffic, sprinted across. One look at the scene was enough — the car half submerged in debris and masses of barbed wire — there was nothing to be done. I didn't know Kenneth Carr, the driver, and was thankful for that. Others arrived quickly. The practice stopped and the ambulance arrived. Not really much of a start to motor racing, I thought.

No practice for the next hour and a half. Then I had another go. The car seemed fine for the first few laps, comfortable but not fast and seeming rather short of revs. Then, suddenly, there was a big bang as the supercharger pressure release valve blew off. Then it did it again, so I came in, reported to Robin and agreed to be ready to have another go early on Monday, the morning of the race, when a mechanic would definitely be available. I'd had a stop watch, on a string, with me in the car and had timed a couple of laps, both at around a hundred and four.

The car and mechanic were both there early on Monday. I told him my findings and his reaction was that "it ought to go faster than that" which, after about half an hour's work, it did.

The Race was number eight in the programme — the Second Whitsun Short Handicap with Lord Howe's Type 59 G.P.Bugatti on Scratch. Starting at the Vickers Shed at the Fork, it was over two complete laps and finishing in the Railway Straight. We were receiving 44 seconds start from Howe but had to give five seconds to both Fleming's Graham Paige, and starts of up to 98 seconds to seven other cars, two of which were non starters. The start was good and the 'Q' Type never missed a beat, with a best lap of just under a hundred and eight despite fairly heavy rain. We left the Graham Paige initially but couldn't hold Fleming and, having at last got moving, Baker came by slowly at the Fork followed by Samuels' 'Q' Type, identical (except for speed!) to ours, so that, in the end, Samuel won at 107.8mph followed by Baker, Fleming and ourselves, Howe being among the non-starters, and none of those who finished ahead being far away.

It was interesting, not exciting as a race, and far, far more comfortable than the same speed on a bike. If I was going to race a car, it would have to be something quite a lot faster. Comfort apart, the big difference was noise. With the engine in front, one was conscious of its noise whereas on a bike, with the engine set low and beneath the fuel tank, one could feel it but not hear it. It was also much more strenuous to control than a car. An interesting, partly enjoyable day.

Meanwhile, quite a lot had been happening on the car front. At the time of the 'MGQ' sortie, I was running a rather racy looking 4½ litre Invicta, a car that I'd bought from Douglas Hawkes of Montlhery fame quite

cheaply because, despite its looks, it was only an average specimen and, one morning when I was enjoying a cup of tea with Arthur Hodge who ran the Esso fuel depot in the paddock, a rather nice Railton drove up and, from it emerged a friend, Dick Wilkins. Dick had raced and owned many lovely cars, including a quick Monza Alfa and later together with Walter Hassan was instrumental in building a a very fast 'special', the BHW later driven at the track by Reg Parnell, the basic of it being the 4.9 litre engine from the ex-Kaye Don Type 54 in a specially built independently sprung chassis, the letters standing for 'Bugatti-Hassan-Wilkins'. At the time, though the Railton was a comparatively recent marque there was growing appreciation of them and they sold well new and secondhand. After extolling its virtue, Dick asked me what I thought of the Invicta, adding that it was a car he'd never owned and always wanted and, when I told him that, from the time I'd first owned one I'd never been without one he suggested we did a swop. I was against it at first because being a friend, he was a great connoisseur of cars and, for all its looks, this particular car was far from the best I'd had. But he was insistent and, in the end, we did a level swop then and there and off he drove in the '4½', knowing my feelings about that particular car. So, apart from some regret at losing my 'open' car in the glorious summer we were having, I felt very happy because, of the two cars, the Railton was the much more marketable.

My pleasure didn't last for long. The car was an early example, good mechanically and very smart but turned out before they'd made an essential modification to the exhaust system so that, even in warm weather one became roasted in just a short run. I don't recall now whether I had to wait for winter weather before selling it but I'm sure I didn't try till the hot spell had ended! Ever since then, when I've seen Dick, he always opens our conversation with "How are you. Been buying any early Railtons recently?" But every cloud has a silver lining and, in trying to sort out the car's problems, I came, first, to know Carol Holbeach, Railton Sales Manager for Thompson & Taylor, the concessionaires whose showrooms were situated in the Brooklands paddock and, subsequently, Capt. (later Sir) Noel Macklin, the head of, first the Invicta company and later, Railton. In fact that particular deal, had I known it at the time, was to change the path of my life before long. It did, to some extent, even at that point because, from then on, I was almost never without a good used Railton among my 'stock' for sale.

Though, from a business point of view, my business car, apart from the Invicta, had to be a saloon or coupe, exciting and sporting cars did come in for resale from time to time and, somewhere around that time, I spotted one nestling unhappily among a number of new cars in the Ford Main Agents in Kingston on Thames — a most unlikely place for a beautiful Speed Six Bentley to be! Appearance wise one couldn't fault it, with its pristine British Racing Green, radiator stoneguard and huge rear-mounted Le Mans type tank, and a short run down the bypass to Esher proved it to be just as good as it looked. But, as one would expect, the price was high so, for the time being, it stayed where it was.

But not for long. A few days later when I was having a drink with Charles Bracken-

The start of a life long love-affair with Invictas. Passenger in Tom Lace's car at Brooklands.

bury in the Club Bar, he said, "By the way, did you know that Ken Waller is selling his Le Mans type Speed Six. It's a good one. You ought to have a look at it. It's probably over at the Flying School now." But it wasn't and I felt sure I knew where it was. I knew Ken Waller by sight and knew that he was a pilot and was to some extent involved in the Brooklands Flying School but, for some strange reason, had never seen the car within the Brooklands perimeter. But thanks, mainly, to Charles who introduced me to him, I bought the car at a much more realistic price. For me, UW4989 became 'Speed Six Number Two', the nicest to drive of all the four I personally owned. There was really nothing to be said against it. Steering and gearchanging were both light, it was fast for a Speed Six, the brakes were good and so was its roadholding. But it was an open car and I already had my own Invicta. I kept it for quite a long time, however, on the basis of "Yes it is for sale — at a price" and was sorry when, later that year, someone did pay the price.

Earlier that year I bought my first two-wheeled 'White Elephant'. Besides Brooklands there were some really great sprint meetings and two of the best were the Brighton Speed Trials held on the seafront and the one held on the quarter mile straight approach road to Gatwick racecourse. Those days were tremendous fun. Just a straight sprint from a standing start through the gears to the finish with no money at the end of it, just a good party afterwards. Eric had always won the 500cc class with his Excelsior with the rest of us yelping at his heels with our Nortons but from the time he had the Brough, he was completely out of reach and had always put up fastest Time of Day, though Noel, with his blown Brough, had several times been a close second.

British motorcycle manufacturers had for long been interested in regaining the World Land Speed Motorcycle Record from Germany and the AJS firm had, some time previously, built a machine specially for the attempt, a 1000cc Vee Twin, the engine of which had chain driven overhead camshafts and a supercharger mounted low down in front of the engine itself. It was never denied that it probably had the speed — the trouble was its handling for, on the information of three different riders, one of

whom it seriously injured, it was labelled a killer and finally consigned to the outer darkness somewhere in the factory. Talking it over together, Jock Forbes and I felt it might be just the thing for a standing start straight quarter Mile or Kilometre and, in the end, I bought it. AJS sold it with some misgivings, warning us of its reputation and pointing out that, in an effort to improve its handling, the supercharger had been removed from its original position and re-sited under the saddle.

In the words of the song sung by Bernard Cribbins: "It did no good — never thought it would". It remained the same terrifying monster it always had been. I tried it first, then Jock, then Noel and we were all agreed. We spent a month experimenting with it noticing at the same time Eric's increasing interest and always maintaining, when he was around, how much improved it was until, one day, to our amazement, he expressed interest in buying it. And buy it he did at really quite a stiff price. Manna from Heaven, literally!

What was in his mind we never knew.

Maybe he thought there were things he could learn from it or maybe he felt he'd like it out of the way. Maybe he thought we really were winning the handling battle. If so he couldn't have paid us a greater compliment. Later, rumour said that half convinced that we were well on the way to solving the problems, he, George Brough and the JAP engine company split the purchase price between them to hold the machine till the Land Speed Record had been broken before consigning it once more to outer darkness. Later still it was said to have ended up in Tasmania but was certainly back in England and on show at the 1985 Brooklands Society Re-union at the track, where its condition was pristine so that, knowing one would never have to battle with it again, it was a pleasure to once again view the scene from its saddle.

Noel Pope was with me when the deal with Eric was agreed, his reaction being "Crikey, that one floated off easily enough. D'you think you could sell the old Anzani?" The Anzani — I'd forgotten that he had it. Another huge 1000cc Vee twin on which

47

Claude Temple had broken World Records and lapped Brooklands at over the century way back in the early and mid 1920's, the British Anzani was a relic of the past even to us. Noel had made his Brooklands debut on it, frightening everyone out of their lives and subsequently being hauled in front of the Stewards for reckless riding. But later it served him well throughout his first season, only being relegated when he bought the blown Brough Superior from Ted Baragwanath.

We did the deal at £15 and though I rather looked forward to a brief ride on the old warrior I didn't get it because, next day when we were lunching together with Franics Beart in the Paddock Cafeteria, Noel said to me "Sold it yet?" "Sold what?" said Francis. "My old Anzani" replied Noel. "Bloody Hell" said Francis, "I didn't know you'd still got it. I'd like to have bought that. Just the thing for Gatwick and Brighton. How much d'you want for it, Charles?" Rather difficult. Both were good friends. "Well, I gave Noel £15. I think that, given time, it'll make £30 because of its history. But, to a friend, how about £25?" Noel said "Disgraceful" and Francis "Of course — and it's obviously clapped after all Noel did to it. Give you sixteen for a quick deal." And he bought it for £20 and later did several sprint meetings with it at Gatwick, from one of which I still have a photograph.

People sometimes say to me today, "Don't you wish you'd kept all those wonderful old bikes and cars. But one doesn't of course. I wasn't master of the big AJS when I was twenty years old so how would I cope with it now I'm seventy plus. We had our fun at the time, were lucky enough to enjoy them as they should be enjoyed and it's nice to go to today's events, seeing not only them again but other, younger, people still enjoying them. At this stage there are no bikes I would want — just half a dozen cars perhaps — I'll list them later and say why.

Nineteen Thirty Six ended with a particularly enjoyable Gatwick Sprint Meeting in September to which we all went to give battle. It was a glorious day and a busy one because one was allowed two runs in each class and if one entered for the higher capacity classes as well as one's own you could be having runs up the course every quarter of an hour if that was what you wanted. And there was one class for Experts and another for Non Experts, the 'Experts' being chaps with specially constructed sprint bikes whereas ours were the ones we used for road and track racing as well. In the 500cc Class, for instance, one was in the 'Non Expert' Class till one had broken the 13 seconds barrier for the standing quarter mile, quite a problem for our bikes in road racing trim and in no way drilled or lightened.

There was quite a lot of skill and some element of luck involved because although the road was straight, it was narrow and steeply cambered towards the sides. Early runs, before the start line became oil spattered and slippery, were best but there was always a queue and it was essential to avoid oil dropped from waiting machines. Later in the day the centre of the start line became unusable and as time passed one had to go nearer and nearer the edge. Rain later in the day could put one right out of the running. This time we fielded the whole 'Brooklands' contingent well fed and victualled — and the results came.

I was rather disappointed to find myself graded as an 'Expert' in the three fifty Class but just pulled off with 14.16secs to Velocette-mounted Eric Oliver's 14.61 and Noel and Francis Beart's Nortons filled the first two places in the 500cc Experts with 13.19 and 13.54. My five hundred pulled off its Experts Barred section and, rather surprisingly came second, with 13.10secs, in the Unlimited Experts to Eric's Brough Superior which netted Fastest Time of Day

The unofficial 'Brooklands Residents Association'. Left to Right: Francis Beart (Norton), A. Sinclair (Mechanic), Jock Forbes (supercharged 1000cc AJS), Charles Mortimer (Standing), F. Baker (Manager to Noel Pope), Noel Pope (Norton). Shortly after this Fernihough bought the big AJS probably to get it out of the way as a rival to his world record attempt.

with 11.80secs. The Club, the Sunbeam M.C.C., always made the last event of the day one for the 'Six Fastest' people of the day and as a result we were all eligible for it if we wanted to be. Eric didn't and, having made F.T.D., packed up and went home but Noel had his 'blown' Brough there and took his place.

Frantic work was going on in the paddock by the end of the day, mainly with chains and engine sprockets to vary gear ratios. Most people were lowering ratios but on one of my previous runs I noticed that one made the last gearchange, from third to top, only about a hundred yards before the finishing line so, bearing in mind the now very slippery start line, I geared 'up', fitting a larger engine sprocket, the idea being to reduce wheelspin at the start and to make only two gear changes, first to second and second to third and hope the engine wouldn't drop a valve before crossing the line; for good measure, I fitted an exhaust megaphone. Megaphones were never used for sprinting since, in theory, they produced no benefit except at maximum revs — which I reckoned my revs were going to be towards the end of the run. Everyone was so busy with their own problems of gearing that they didn't notice I'd changed mine — but they all had something rude to say about the megaphone. But the laughs died when my good old five hundred won the class with 13.02secs to Noel's Brough mounted

13.27secs, after which we all adjourned to that nice pub, the Chequers at Horley.

The last quarter of 1936 had produced record sales, including the Le Mans Bentley 'Speed Six' and stock consisted mainly of good 'traded in' Railtons, a Morris Minor '£100 New' two-seater and a quarter share in an early Austin Seven Chummy which cost me £1 and led to an unpleasant sequel. This was Noel's fault in every way. It was he who found the Austin, selling three quarters of it at £1 a time to Francis Beart, Works Triumph rider Freddy Clark and myself. For quite some time we all used it for 'internal' runs within the track's perimeter, the driving becoming more and more furious as the poor little car became more and more tired of life. One regular trip that we did with it was made after bike meetings, from the Paddock to enjoy the company of the Brooklands Aero Club bar on the Byfleet side of the track, a journey of about a mile. The end came when returning on the evening of the 1936 Hutchinson 100, all four of us rather 'well tuned' and fortunately, with no traffic on the Aerodrome road, Francis, who was driving it as fast as the Austin would go but quite sensibly, had Noel beside him with Fred and I enjoying the evening air in the back. Suddenly Noel said "Look, there's a haystack beside the road — charge it". Turning towards it, Francis then thought better of it whereupon Noel grabbed the steering wheel which promptly broke off the column, the result being that the front wheels swung hard to the right, the nearside rear collapsing and the car going end over end down the road and finishing on top of us. Net result: Francis a broken finger, Fred a broken collar-bone and Noel and I with multiple cuts from the shattered plate glass windscreen which joined us wrapped in the aged hood. In retrospect it did seem so stupid to have had that sort of accident only two hours after completing a 100 mile blind on the track

proper. The doctors and staff of Weybridge hospital thought so too, even though we didn't admit to the cause of the 'prang'. And with hindsight, rather a sad end to what would have been a valuable car today!

Browsing throught the *Autocar* of October 9th that year I saw among the 'Specially Selected' used car section a picture of an absolutely suberb 'Speed Six' Bentley Coupe offered by Francis Radford of South Kensington with the description 'Speed Six Bentley Special Streamline Coupe by Gurney Nutting built to the order of a World famous racing motorist. Recently overhauled, numerous extras, indistinguishable from new. £395.' The price killed it from the aspect of re-sale and I though no more about it. Later I learned that the 'famous racing motorist' was Woolf Barnato, Chairman of Bentley Motors, and that the car was said to have raced the 'Blue Train' across France, though I don't recall hearing that until after the war. That was my first meeting with GJ3811 and all I could do at the time was to hope that, one day, maybe when she was older, there'd be another.

Then, as now, both the Motorcycle Show and the Motor Show were events not to be missed each Autumn, the first especially because not only was it a great social occasion but also because at that time of year one was thinking of the next year's racing in terms of money-raising and any possible help that could be screwed out of hard-bitten manufacturers, fuel and oil companies and accessory firms. That year, the second successful one for me, some of the latter were more interested and slightly less non-commital than previously, partly because of the successful record-breaking run Eric and I had done with the Cotton and 'my' fuel and oil suppliers, Esso, had promised an early contract for 1937.

The Motor Show was interesting and enjoyable as well because at this stage, apart from seeing all the new cars first hand, one was always looking ahead in terms of new business contacts. In the 1930's there was another event, the Used Car Motor Show, held at the time of the Motor Show proper though not connected with it in any way and, to me this was even more interesting with its wide variety of cars, many of them with low mileages and others earlier but still in pristine condition. This was held in a large hall in Islington and, as usual, I went along again in search of bargains. I only found one that year, not a bargain in terms of price but one that, somehow, I just had to have. Strolling round slowly and taking it all in as I went, I came across one sporting a large placard proclaiming it 'The Car of the Year': and there, in all her glory, stood GJ3811, the Speed Six Bentley Coupe, pristine in all her glory but looking not entirely happy in such surroundings. A glimpse of the descriptive label on her windscreen showed that not only was she still the property of the South Kensington firm of France Radford whose advertisement I'd first seen but that, also, her price had been reduced from £345 to £275. Hope springs eternal and I made underground tracks to South Kensington straight away.

Strangely, I don't have clear memories of the negotiations I had with Basil Radford, whom I was meeting for the first time. I know I introduced myslf as a dealer in cars that were hard to sell so that he would know not only that I was serious but also 'realistic' pricewise. I recall my first offer of £200 being turned down and a long and friendly discussion following which ended with me thanking him and making my way to the door. Literally as it closed, he stood up and said "Right. How about £-?" but I'm not sure of the figure — I think it must have been £225. A condition of sale was that she had to stay on show for the remainder of the exhibition, though with a 'Sold' ticket on her windscreen and I know that I paid another visit to the Show before the day came to collect her.

On the day she behaved perfectly, starting at the first touch of the button and filtering impeccably through London's traffic as though she had done it all before, which I expect she had. Once on the Kingston Bypass I gave her her head and she responded at once, running easily up to between seventy five and eighty and between Chessington and Leatherhead she seemed happier the faster she went, though not quite as happy under fairly heavy braking on the downhill stretch approaching Leatherhead.

That run was the start of a love affair that lasted until the outbreak of war in 1939 even though, on the road, she wasn't as nice a car to drive as the open Le Mans replica four-seater with its light steering, gearchange and good roadholding.

Nineteen Thirty Seven came in with a hiccup. A new contract from Reg Tanner, Competition Manager of Esso offered as promised, better terms, but was different because it also advised that, as with the other fuel and oil suppliers, they would be transferring their support from Brooklands to the T.T. in the Isle of Man, though they would also give support to Record Breaking. My dear old mother still had the same fear of the Island so the options were (1) To continue at Brooklands without the help of Bonus, (2) To do the Bonus-sponsored specified events, preparing and looking after the machines myself and finding someone to ride them or (3) to switch from bikes to cars.

It wasn't too difficult to opt for number two. I'd known Jock Forbes since we were students together at the College of Automobile Engineering way back in the early 1930's, ridden against him and socialised with him. We were two of a group who spent a lot of time together and when I sounded him out, he was keen on the idea as I was. So for 1937 our stable consisted of his five hundred Norton, my five hundred and three fifty and a brand new racing two fifty Excelsior 'Manxman', all the Nortons going back to the factory for overhaul and updating.

The planned progrmme was a busy one: all the main Brooklands events including the Mountain Championship, 100 Miles Grand Prix and Hutchinson 100 Mile Race and whatever smaller races we could fit in with, in additon, the 'North West 200' in Ireland, a Donington meeting or two and the Isle of Man in June. Despite our friendship, the partnership could have foundered right at the start and, had it done so, it would have been my fault. As usual, the factory did us proud and all three bikes came back after Christmas well ahead of schedule and ready to test. With the factory's rather reluctant agreement one job had been left undone on the three fifty: the original well-worn oil scavenge pump had been left. We had discovered previously that new and unworn scavenge pumps took some time to free off and that this slowed the engine by absorbing power as the pump on this engine was more than usually free running — so free in fact that if left overnight oil would run from the tank supply line down to the pump and even through it and fill the crankcase. So, cunningly, we fitted a tap at the base of the tank even though this meant turning it on before starting the engine and, due to excep-tional circumstances, this boomeranged later. The Excelsior arrived so late that we only had time to have a quick look round it before setting off for Donington and though half a dozen outer circuit Brooklands laps showed it to be well up performance wise there was no time to go further, so that when leading the 250cc race it slowed half way through and only finished third due to the air lever being badly fitted at the works, closing and having to be held open for half the race. My fault, I should have put in some overtime and checked everything properly.

Much worse befell us in Ireland. Jock had ridden previously in the 'North West 200', the Organising Committee were delighted to see him and even more so when they heard that it was my first visit. With typical Irish hospitality, they put on a great party, so much so that, before it ended, we agreed only to practice with the five hundred next morning. Quite how we ever got to the start I don't know. Jock took the car up to the start and I rode the bike and once the field had set off I went back to try and recover, lying down in the car. Some minutes later I heard them returning but couldn't spot Jock as they passed. Lap two and I was sure he wasn't among them so I went to Race Control where they told me the engine had seized out on the course but that he was alright. I couldn't understand it — Nortons never seized. Some time later he arrived back in a course car and jumped out brandishing an axe and shouting ''Where's my sponsor — Ah, there he is.''

What had happened? Well, though by then I knew every nut and bolt on each of the three Nortons, I had, in my hungover state not only given him the wrong bike, the three fifty instead of the five hundred but, believing it to be the five hundred, had ridden it to the start and given it to him with the oil supply tap turned off, not even noticing it on the way to the circuit! But, thank Heaven, the season went smoothly from then — and we fitted a new three fifty scavenge pump on returning home, plus big end and main bearings and piston. The barrel, fortunately, responded to honing, which highlighted the excellent quality of Norton materials.

Though my only rides that year were when testing, I thoroughly enjoyed it all. Jock, much smaller and lighter than I, put up better performances and improved on nearly all my previous winning times. At the Gatwick Speed Trials, his winning time of 13.87secs with the three fifty won the class and missed the class record by a hundredth

Not a 'Manx' Norton but the road going 'International' version. Fitted with a Manx tank and a different piston it lapped the outer circuit at 100.6mph and won at least 2 races. But it did not handle like a Manx and vibrated violently through the handlebars at speed.

of a second. He won the same Class at the Brighton Speed Trials on the same three fifty I'd won with in the previous year at a speed three miles an hour faster and won the Senior Mountain Championship as well and finished third in the Hutchinson 100.

As we were packing up the pit equipment after the finish of the race we were visited by a Steward of the meeting he told us that as the silencer of the second man's machine had shed its fishtail two laps before the end we were entitled to put in a protest which would be upheld. Without asking who the second man had been, Jock said "I'm only the rider, it's up to my entrant". I'd noticed

it and was going to tell him any case but was glad to be able to waive it. Well as I knew Jock socially, there were things that I learned about his riding: though he was equally competitive at Brooklands with all three classes of bike, he preferred the two fifty and three fifty to the five hundred. When we went to the Island in June we had a full week of practice so, with a thirty seven mile circuit, we devised a schedule of using one machine a day, the first session consisting of a single lap, the second of two laps and the third of three consecutive laps.

We had no problems with the two fifty or three fifty but he complained of bad handling on the five hundred during the third lap of the session though even Nortons could find nothing wrong with the bike.

We had no problems in the Junior Race, the three fifty getting a Silver Replica and finishing well up for a privately entered machine against mainly trade entries but, in the Senior, Jock was complaining bitterly about handling when he came in to fill at the end of Lap 3. I urged him to pack it up but he insisted on continuing but, in the end, did retire with 'handling problems' at the end of lap four. Bearing in mind all the facts I thought I knew what the trouble was. In winning the Mountain Championship prior to going to the Island Jock had broken the 500cc Mountain Lap Record so after putting the bike under wraps for a week after our return — in disgrace as it were, — I waited until he was away one morning, cleaned the bike down to the last nut and bolt and, when he returned, asked him to take it out on the same circuit. I said that I'd done some work to it which just might transform the handling

adding that, in fact, I felt pretty sure that it would. The result was that after one cruising lap, he reeled off five, all of which broke the record he'd broken a month or two earlier. Subsequently he often urged me to tell him the changes I'd made but I never could because besides having carried out no mods, I knew what the trouble was — with his small size, the big 'un became too tiring a proposition for him in a race of the type and length of the T.T. What I did, though, was to swing him away from the five hundred in the 1938 T.T., and that worked wonders in the Lightweight and Junior T.T.'s and, to this day, he won't know unless, of course, he reads this!

I found that I loved the Island, though I wouldn't want to live there and, in the autumn that year, went over for the Manx Grand Prix, the amateur version of the T.T., this time with my girl friend and in the Bentley. Good as the Isle of Man Steam Packet Company always was, one look at GJ3811 made them say that the car was too

Jock Forbes who rode the authors machines in the Isle of Man. Charles having promised his mother he would never ride there. This Norton is oddly set up, having a megaphone exhaust for the 'Island' but a brakeless front wheel for Brooklands outer circuit. Probably about to be given a final 'squirt' down the Aerodrome road before departure for the Isle of Man.

big for the 'Mona's Isle'; it would have to follow next day on the cargo boat. There were no 'Drive on-Drive Offs' then of course and at that stage of the tide access from quay to boat was by two unconnected ramps each roughly two feet wide and with a gradient of about one in two. Personally I would have been happier for it to have been cargo but, thinking she was helping, Strelsa prevailed on the dock foreman and the First Mate to let us try, so with some concern for the clutch, ground clearance at the top and whether the brakes would hold it if all else failed, we made one successful attempt. But, even then our troubles weren't over. The car was athwart ship and had to be turned, which was done with garage jacks with swivelling wheels. By the time this operation had been carried out, the deck planking had suffered, much to the dismay of the Mate. On arrival at Douglas, the whole procedure had to be carried out in reverse, even to reversing down the ramp which, with the car's rather poor rearward visibility, wasn't easy. But, in the end, it was well worth it even though it had to be the cargo boat back to Liverpool.

It was around this time that I had the most frightening trip of all. Charles Brackenbury and I had planned to go up to Donington in the Bentley to see the Works Auto Unions and Mercedes Benz Grand Prix cars in action, but the day before the race he rang up to say that he was with Count Heydon, the Delahaye Concessionaire and that as Heydon was also going, it would surely be better if we all three went in his 2/4 Seater Delahaye Coupe which would be faster, more economical and more comfortable than the Bentley. We met at seven o'clock next morning at the Ship Hotel at Weybridge, the party consisting of Charles, Heydon, a friend of his, Jose Dibos, and myself. The car turned out to be the latest — and fastest — Delahaye, pristine and beautiful. Charles sat in the front with Dibos

and I in the back and as we set off Charles turned to us saying that as the back was a bit cramped, we'd change places at half distance. Heydon was a tremendous character, a non-stop talker always armed with a seemingly endless fund of amusing stories and Charles was always a good foil for him. But some idea of what the trip was going to be like was gathered instantly when we topped eighty miles an hour by the end of Weybridge High Street.

We were lucky for the first hour and a half, there wasn't much traffic about, but the closer we got to Donington the thicker it became and all one could do was to try and console oneself with the thought that at least it would be a quick trip with plenty of alternative transport on the way home. Time and time again we passed lines of eight or ten cars coming in the opposite direction. Then it happened. A long straight with a gradual left hand curve in the distance and this time about twelve cars to pass. Till then the opposing motorists had been content to brake and flash their lights — but here was one cast in a different mould. The gap narrowed as the speedometer indicated a hundred — there was a tremendous crash — and we were through, a roar of laughter from Heydon with "Dibos we got 'im — you hear de smack" and we were continuing faster than ever, not even stopping further down the road to inspect the extent of the damage. Needless to say we were recovering in the Paddock Bar well before the pubs were open. Damage to the car was a rear off-side wing nearly torn off and with the wing mainly attached with wire we had a better journey home with Charles driving. A day to remember.

The Barnato Coupe had quite a long rest after this because among other cars bought was an extremely handsome Speed Six Barker-bodied boat-tailed two-seater, the actual car that had been the centrepiece of the Barker Stand at the 1929 Motor Show.

In an article that Dennis May wrote in the *Autocar* of October 27th 1944, he said "Seldom, probably, has quite such a lot of motorcar been bought for as little as £35. At the 1929 Motor Show this actual boat-bodied Bentley had put a posse of carpenters to the trouble of sawing chunks out of the perimeter of the stand to make room for the far-flung extremities of its streamlined wings. With its long, gleaming panorama of bonnet forrard and mahogany decked locker aft, between them sandwiched the contrastingly brief 'inhabited locality', the car was an eye-catcher wherever it went. The performance of PK9460, as befitted its advancing years and mileage, was well down on the two other Coupes and the Le Mans four-seater, a fact for which, in a way, Mort was not ungrateful."

All true and though initially I did feel that it was 'one to keep' instead of GJ3811, one only had to use it daily for a bit to know which one to keep. I did buy it privately for £35 and well recall its sale for one reason. It had been advertised for sale in one of the weekly journals priced at £75, for with that type and size of car one knew tht its sale would centre on price negotiation. No replies had followed the ad when, one lunchtime, I got a call from a private buyer down in Swansea, the gist of which was that if I would set off then and there and arrive at his hotel in Swansea by seven that evening, he would pay me sixty five pounds for the car, dine me well and put me up for the night. Payment would be in cash. Rather a problem in that he might or might not be a time waster. We talked for a bit, my line being that how could he say that about a car he'd never seen? "I'm going on your advertised description. If the car is as you describe, I'll have it." So I set off. No motorways in those days and the nearer I got to Wales, the worse the weather became, ending in heavy snow for the last twenty miles. One reason I particularly remember the deal was that, wondering for most of the way whether I was victim of a time waster or even a leg-pull, I arrived at the Hotel, which was huge, with a long flight of marble steps up to its swing door to find a tall man walking down towards the car pulling out 'fivers' from his trouser pocket as he came. A man of his word, in fact. And that concluded the year 1937.

The start of 1938 was a period of indecision and decision. The International scene looked so bleak that it seemed hardly worthwhile bothering about car racing, let alone bikes. But in the end Jock and I decided to go ahead with a programme which included the Isle of Man in June, after which we would disband and I would switch to cars. All that 'half season' was good, the Island

The fourth of the authors Speed Six Bentleys. This one was disappointingly slow and felt unhappy at over 80mph. It was the actual 1929 Motor Show car and so long that they had to dismantle the stand to get it on.

particularly, for we got Silver Replicas in both the Lightweight and Junior T.T.'s, the latter with the first of the 'spring frame' Nortons bought specially for the race though, for reasons of sentiment, I still kept my old rigid frame three fifty. Of the two bikes we had in the Island, the little Excelsior acquitted itself best, finishing on the leader board and being the second private entry to come home, Maurice Cann pipping us by just a few seconds. We sold both bikes before going home — and that was that.

Back home, I had lunch with Charles Brackenbury. I said "Charles, I want to get a good, reliable racing car with a maximum of not less than a hundred and twenty. I'd like to get it fairly soon and can spend up to £250." He said "Then buy Andrew Leitch's Type 35B Bugatti. You won't have to spend all your money. Keiller, of Keiller's marmalade, had it first but didn't race it. Then Jock Leith had it and raced it, then

Charlie Martin, then Andrew. I've test driven it quite a lot. Bill Langrish has been the only one to look after it. It had a bit of a shunt, I think it was in Ireland when Jock had it. It was properly repaired and re-aligned after that but has been a bit of a bastard on the Outer Circuit ever since. The nearside rear wheel and offside front both have cracks but so do many Type 35's and 51's. The scrutineers have diagrams of both cracks in their folios and neither have crept up to this season. Nothing wrong with it unless you want to use it on the Outer. Try him at £125."

I did, after a short chat with Bill Langrish who'd known and looked after the car for the whole of its racing life, first to make sure he'd be willing to continue doing so and also to see whether there was anything against it that Charles didn't know, which was unlikely because, at that time he'd driven virtually every Bugatti regularly running at

Jock Forbes on the author's 250cc Excelsior. Charles always believed him to be at his best on small machines.

Brooklands and had raced quite a few of them.

Andrew put on a very good show of horror at the idea of £125. "A hundred and twenty five? No, no, no, it's worth double that to anyone" and lauched into a diabtribe of its history. "Andrew, I know all that. If it wasn't for that I wouldn't want to have a go at it. Look at the facts. it's old and obsolete, there's no record of when the crank was re-rollered so that could go at any time. It must be bent or it would be as good as the others on the outer circuit. It's use is limited even at Brooklands, its days are numbered and when I was looking at it the other day, I found that two and maybe all the wheels are cracked." And in the end, we did a deal at £150.

I still recall the first practice I had with it — on a weekday and on the Mountain circuit. Though Andrew was a giant, everything seemed to fit and when Bill had run through the starting procedure, I set off.

He and I knew each other well because from time to time he used to come to the bike meetings. Charles was 'technically' in charge and I did ten laps, each a bit faster than the one before and when I came in found that the best was faster than Andrew or Jock Leith's but not really near to Charlie Martin's. That was all I felt I needed to do — the car had behaved perfectly and there seemed no point in continuing to wear the poor old thing out.

Though I did want to do some sprints as well as races, I wasn't keen to use the car for those, mainly because of the stresses sprinting put on a car but also because its age prevented it being really competitive against the later ERAs, Maseratis and Altas. Robin Jackson, who had virtually loaned me the 'Q' Type Midget a year earlier, now had a single seater supercharged Alta and I began to wonder whether I dared ask him about that. When at last I did, he was immediately enthusiastic and agreed not only to lend me

The 2.3 litre Type 35B Bugatti at the Dunlop Jubilee Meeting. Followed by Fay Taylour (Bugatti Type 35B), Ansell ERA and McClure 2 litre Riley.

the car but also to lay on, free of charge, the services of a mechanic and transporter as well for the first event, the Brighton Speed Trials, held along the seafront in July that year, though later they were always in September.

I spent a morning at Brooklands with the car and with the same mechanic I'd had with the 'Q' type, mainly practising standing starts with, alternately, single and twin rear wheel. My first and lasting impressions, despite owning it later and despite my later friendship and admiration for Geoffrey Taylor, its designer, were of dislike, particularly of its inability to transmit engine power to the road. In retrospect, I may perhaps be guilty of drawing too close a comparison to the Bugatti which had a much lower power to weight ratio but whereas the '2.3' exuded quality, the Alta seemed to me the opposite. This and the fact that whereas the Bugatti never displayed temperament,

the Alta frequently did.

But I had to admit that, on the day at Brighton, it behaved reasonably well — it was just one of its better days or maybe it was awed by the presence of the mechanic! It rained all day — the worst weather possible for the car. The 1½ Litre Racing Car Class was quite well supported with a cast ranging from 'Specials' up to Altas and ERAs, the latter being led by Earl Howe's Zoller blow car. From previous knowledge of Brighton I knew that with entries being set off in pairs, the nearside of the start line was always more slippery than the sea side and made a mental note to make sure of not getting it. Our paddock bay was next to Howe's and when the time came to go to the start line, the 'Old Man' said "Shall we go together then?" to which I replied "Sure", not noticing how quickly he jumped into the cockpit so as to be head of the queue. The Alta followed bad temperedly,

With the 1½ litre Alta at the 1938 Brighton Speed Trials.

noting the 'Old Man's' quick right turn on reaching the line. Our side wasn't just wet — there was a shimmering torrent of water running across it, so much so that it seemed better to start in second gear rather than first. In the circumstances our start was quite good, even though the Old Man with his 'ZF' non-slip rear axle pulled away easily — and that was it. But when, a little later in the day, the results of all runs were known, we were delighted to find Howe the winner of the class with ourselves second and Hugh Hunter's Alta third.

Our 'Press' was quite good also and with a photograph of the two cars getting away, the *Motor* said "Then Earl Howe got going with the 1½ litre ERA and with a tremendous getaway despite the unpleasant conditions immediately established a new Record for 1500cc Racing Cars. Mortimer was a very good second and H.C. Hunter did a good run only decimal points behind him." In retrospect, I don't recall the holder of the time for the record but, all things considered, it must have been done in similar conditions or by a very slow car! To break it in those conditions just goes to show what a fine driver 'The Old Man' was.

Robin was pleased about this and came himself to the next one, the Lewes Speed Trials, held on the nearly straight but very bumpy and steep private approach road to Lewes Race Course on August 20th. Our main opposition, this time, came from Peter Monkhouse's ERA, as strong a challenge as Howe's if not stronger because besides being a director of a tuning business, Peter was rather a specialist in sprinting. Initially the Alta refused to run on all four cylinders but Robin quickly cured that and it won the 1½ Litre Racing Class with 20.36secs to the ERA's 20.72. Running in the 2 Litre Class it began misfiring again, this time when actually on the line so that there was no time left to deal with it but, despite that, we did come second to Peter with 20.75secs but despite

Robin's efforts it was well 'off song' for the Racing Cars Unlimited, though even in that Class it came fourth, beating most of the entry.

Back to Brooklands and the first outing with the Bugatti at the Dunlop Jubilee Meeting on September 24th, rather a Star occasion to mark the 50th Anniversary of Dunlop with a plushy programme of ten races including a seven lap Outer Circuit one for the Dunlop Jubilee Cup with the big 8 Litre Barnato Hassan, driven by Oliver Bertram on Scratch, two 'Ecurie Bleu' 4½ Litre, twelve cylcinder Delahayes for Dreyfus and Comotti and Wimille with a three litre, twelve cylinder Alfa Romeo among others.

Being young and still fairly impressionable, all this went rather deeply with me and I would really have preferred to make my four wheeled debut at a rather less star-studded meeting, particularly as Wimille and his Alfa were on the Scratch mark in my race, the first Dunlop Road Handicap, on the Campbell Circuit. My doubts centred round two aspects of the thing, the first being that while, by that time, I knew quite a lot about Brooklands and its handicapping system and geography, I didn't really know the car and had never even driven or ridden round the Campbell Circuit. And I was a bit concerned about passing procedure with a car, though I knew it from beginning to end with a bike. One could weave a bike through a crowded field with no problems, aiming for the largest gap available and, since one had no rearview mirror, totally unconcerned about the problems of a faster rider aiming to pass just as you were about to pass another ahead. it was 'everyone for himself' so to speak.

But with a car, and a rear view mirror, it became a problem of 'one eye on the road and the other on the mirror' and, on my debut, I didn't want to receive Jean Pierre astern just as I was in the middle of what

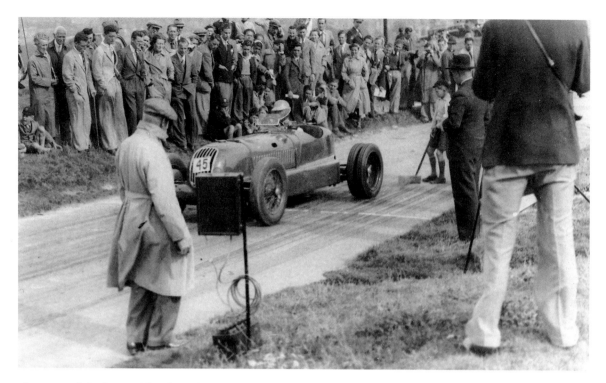

A successful day with the Alta at Lewes in 1938 winning the class and beating the ERAs.

seemed to me an excellent bit of passing. It really was rather a problem — one had become so used to 'first come — first served.'

I drove the Bugatti for the first time a week or so before the meeting, not on the Campbell Circuit but first on the Mountain circuit and then on the Outer. There were no problems though, due to vibration, it was quite impossible to get a clear picture in the mirror — one would only know if there was another car astern. Bill Langrish outlined starting procedure, aided by a friend, Roger Acland, who subsequently always came along in an unpaid capacity — and always had with the car's previous owners. I didn't plan to set the world on fire then — only to get to know as much as possible about the car. The Bugatti gearchange, 1st left and back, 2nd left and forward, 3rd right and back and Top right and forward took almost no getting used to and the faster one went,

the smaller the car seemed, the Mountain Lap time out of ten being one minute two seconds, sixty seven point nine three miles an hour, five seconds slower than the best I'd done on a bike — so there was much room for improvement since Charlie Martin was said to have done fifty six seconds during his span of ownership.

Then, despite warnings, I had a 'go' on the Outer, ten laps in all with a best of one minute twenty four seconds, a hundred and eighteen mph, which decided me that rumour was right — there was no fun to be had there.

With the feeling that I now felt happy with the car I did only five laps practice on the Campbell circuit on the day before the race. Knowing the Brooklands handicapping system inside out, there was no point in hustling right from the start. Newcomers were always rather stiffly handicapped on their first appearance and there was no point

in bursting oneself first time out — one had seen it happen many times previously without success and I wanted, then, to learn more about both car and the circuit and to make the first big effort on the Mountain circuit which I did know, so on that first 'official' Road circuit outing, I was happy with two minutes, four seconds — 65.82mph.

The 'First Dunlop Road Handicap' produced seventeen entries, or eighteen according to the programme because number thirteen was never included in Brooklands programmes. There must have been some non-starters and Wimille was certainly among them for Johnny Wakefield, whose ERA was down to receive fifteen seconds start from him, was on the scratch mark as we lined up for the five lap 'dice'.

I was glad about that because before switching to cars, Johnny had been racing at the track with Nortons at the same time as I, and we knew each other well. His race number was '2' and mine '10' and I received thirty one seconds from him — 5.2 seconds a lap — so I reckoned he'd catch me. The 'Limit' car, Dorothy Stanley Turner's 'Q' Type supercharged Midget received one minute two seconds from Johnny and thirty one seconds from me.

Strangely, very few memories of that race remain, the main one being of traffic congestion on the last lap as everyone seemed to be trying to get by everyone else but the good old Bugatti was classified fifth finisher with a best lap of two minutes one, sixty seven point four five mph. And according to Bill Boddy's 'History of

Brooklands', Johnny Wakefield won it at 71.59mph with George Harvey Noble's Maserati 6C driven by Peter Aitken second and Hanson's similar car third.

My main recollection of that meeting was that, with my race being Number 5 on the card, not enjoying races 1 to 4 as I usually did and enjoying numbers 6 to 10 far more.

The gap between that meeting on September 24th and the next and final one that year, on October 15th was spent partly in trading and partly with a Devon holiday with my dear old mother transported in GJ3811, the Speed Six 'Barnato' Coupe.

I learned a lot at that October Meeting, again on the Campbell Road Circuit and over five laps. Sixteen entries this time with Ian Connell's and Johnny's ERA's, Lord Avebury's, Beadle's and Hanson's Altas, Torin's 8C Maserati and Ashby's Monoposto Alfa Romeo all non-starters, I found myself handicapped to go from the same mark as Count Heyden's 3½ Litre Delahaye driven by ex-motorbike racer Charlie Dodson, receiving twenty seven seconds start from Count Lurani's Scuderia Ambrosiana type 6C Maserati and Reg Parnell's 4.9 Litre BHW. Expert as he was then with cars, Charlie made a superb start but, quite quickly I found that I could stay right with him and, given a lap or two, might by able to get by. But brought up in a hard school, he knew all the answers and each time I tried, he used the verges at corners, showering the poor old 35B with earth and stones though, at the finish we were still close behind. Bob Ansell's ERA won at 69.16mph, with Percy Maclure's Riley 4/5th of a second behind, the Delahaye third and ourselves fourth with a best lap of 68.01mph.

The End of One Era . . .

Time, once more, to take stock and form a plan for 1939. Like the British Motor Cycle Racing Club, the B.A.R.C. runners competed for an aggregate award each season, the prize being a cup presented by the 'Daily Mirror'. Scoring was by a points system, 8 points for a win, 7 for second place, 6 for third down to one point for eighth, so that the first essential was to start in as many short races as possible in a season. So ideally one needed more than one car. A bit of a problem when it had been rather a stretch to buy even one! But it was the right time of year with no more racing and the winter ahead in which to amass funds and then — back to Brackenbury for guidance. Charles never failed. This time also, it was a car that one knew. Everyone, in fact, knew the Bellevue Garage, run by the Evans family and managed by W. E. (Wilkie) Wilkinson.

Charles said "Talk to Wilkie. Bellevue are selling the Magnette 1100cc single seater. You know it. It started as a 'N' Type. Ugly car. Body offset to the right like Dobb's 2 litre Riley, almost entirely 'K.3' now, classified 'KN', unblown and with six Amal carburettors." I did know it and invested another £150 in it.

The 'KN' was in all respects a 'poor man's' racing car, immaculate, ugly as Charles had said and impeccably maintained in the Evans tradition. Not fast — Wilkie thought it 'ought to lap at a hundred' and ideal for short handicaps. One that I felt capable of maintaining on my own particularly because the six Amal carburettors were the same type

as we'd had on bikes.

The car came with the full documentation. Bore 57mm. Stroke 71mm. Capacity 1087cc. Max R.P.M. 6500. Oil Pressure 100-120lbs. Fuel Tank Pressure 2lbs. Fuel Esso MG2. Oil Castor Base. Rear Axle Duckhams 'Keenol'. Plugs KLG 646. Weight with tank empty 1286lbs or 11½cwt. Chassis Number NA.0756. Engine No. 1013.AN, and plenty more besides. Larger tyres at the back than on the front for the outer circuit and all one had to do for the Mountain and Road Circuits was to change them over, back to front so to speak.

The only small 'less good' feature was that the ratio between second and third was rather wide — nothing else. 'Wilkie' was there for the first test in early May. Initial slight misfiring was cured by removing and cleaning all six carburettors and, on the Mountain Circuit, some front wheel patter was cured by front shock absorber adjustment, giving an outer circuit lap speed on ninety seven and a Mountain lap time of one minute seven — (62.86mph). Tested on the Mountain circuit later that day, the Bugatti came out of hibernation well, knocking two seconds off its 1938 best with one minute (70.20mph).

March 11th opened the 1939 season rather quickly because the Magnette was in the first Outer circuit race of the day. Handicapped to start from the same mark as G.L. Baker's 5 litre Graham Page, it did its best, lapping at 99.01mph, but despite slight improvement by using a slightly higher

The rather ugly modified offset KN M.G. Magnette fitted with six motorcycle Amal carburettors. With it the author won the first Whitsun Handicap in 1939. If you leant out too far you burned your left elbow.

line on the bankings, that wasn't good enough and it finished unplaced, Ian Connell's big four litre Daraccq winning at 111.49mph.

Race 6, The Second March Mountain Handicap, was better for the little car with a fourth place, five aggregate points scored and a best lap of one minute five (64.80mph). The handicap for the Bugatti in Race 8, the Third March Mountain Handicap looked rather more realistic this time and, after talking it over with Charles, Bill and Roger it was decided to have a rather strong 'go' once we'd all managed to get money on with the Bookmakers. Though it did turn out alright, it was a matter of 'only just' because despite an average of 69.74mph and a best lap of 72.62mph, Reg Parnell's big '4.9' BHW in second place was only forty yards behind at the finish!

The next Meeting, Easter Monday on April 10th, was good also. In the Second Easter Road Handicap with George Abecassis Alta and Wakefield's ERA on Scratch, the Bugatti had twenty five seconds start in five laps from Percy Maclure's 1½ litre supercharged Riley which, with its independent front suspension and 1½ litre blown six cyclinder engine was an ERA in all but name despite its derivation so that, in the end, Percy won with the Bugatti just 5.6 seconds astern in second place, 'Perce' averaging 70.72 to our 67.11mph. But it was the Magnette that swung the day in the end, winning the First Easter Mountain Handicap at 66.23mph by 2.4 secs from Aldington's works two litre Frazer Nash-BMW who had conceded us five seconds in five laps. One knew that this must be a very open race because, other threats apart, Aldington was enormously experienced,

65

The KN Magnette followed by faster machinery. Being offset it always felt better cornering to the right.

knew his car inside out and had had years of Brooklands experience and many successes. His car was more modern, was 2 litres to our 1100cc and had independent suspension to our 'cart springs'!

The Magnette ws already obsolete but was light, held the track well on corners and its offset body to the right gave one the feeling that one could get round a right hander at any speed. But in this race its big handicap was going to be not only its smaller capacity in getting quickly away from the start line but, far more, the handicap of the wide gap between second and third gear ratios and though we felt there was a chance of a win we weren't all that confident and thought that the race result would be decided during the first lap. Though only a run-of-the-mill short Brooklands handicap it was exciting for us both and, so we were told, for the spectators. Looking in the mirror on the way down from the Members Bridge to the Chronograph Villa Hairpin on Lap one, the FN-BMW was very slightly further behind than one had expectd but, throughout the

five laps it crept up steadily and relentlessly developing into a situation where, first, one had to lead round the hairpin on the last lap and, secondly, get round it a bit faster than on any previous lap because once the car behind had rounded, its extra capacity would tell on the straight run in. Everything went exactly right. Our best previous lap, number three, was 68.38mph. The last, at 69.05mph was, I believe, slightly the best the car had done in that form and just showed, really, the margin of safety that was there. It was small stuff but good fun.

Had I known it at the time, the next Brooklands Meeting, Whitsun on May 29th was the last car meeting at which I was to drive. By that time I led the Aggregate competition fairly easily with 28 points, followed by Reg Parnell with 20, Ian Connell with 19 and Peter Aitken with 18, all for the Campbell and Mountain circuits of course, while C.G.H. Dunham and Bob Gerard dead heated for the Outer Circuit Aggregate with 23 points each. In the Second Five Lap Whitsun Road Handicap Reg had 28 seconds start

A fine action shot by Louis Klemantski of the Bugatti on the Brooklands Road Circuit in 1939.

from the Scratch man, 'Jock' Horsfall in his ERA and with the Magnette, I had one minute twenty two seconds and saw Reg as a very likely winner — to the extent of putting money on him with Jack Linton with whom I usually dealt. On the start line Reg said "Who carries your money on this one, Charles?" and when I told him he did, he laughed and said that I carried his. With a big time gap between us, it wasn't until half way through the last lap that I saw him in the mirror, fairly steaming up. By that time I led the race but as I lined up for the last left hander over the river Wey, I heard a dreadful noise and saw Reg pass, going backwards among a cloud of dust and flying stones so that, in the end, I won.

When, later in the afternoon, we met, side-by-side on the start line of the First Mountain Handicap, I said "Thanks for the present, Reg. Are you going to give me this one as well?" He replied "No, no presents this time. I'm having this one — definitely." I quite agreed because, that time I was getting only three seconds start from him with the Bugatti in five laps — 2.3 aged litres versus 4.9 modernised. Though my fastest lap was the best I'd ever done — 56 seconds (75.21mph), Reg did get me on the last lap and so did four others including Jock Horsfall who won at 77.15mph. It was a fast race by almost any standards.

There was quite a lot to think about at this stage. My best lap on the Mountain Circuit with the Bugatti had equalled Charlie Martin's when he had owned the car and was substantially better than those of previous owners of the car. It could never

be made competitive against ERAs and Maseratis, neither of which I could afford, the options seemed to be either to sell it and save for a faster car or potter on and collect 'seconds' and 'thirds' with never a hope of a win. I now led the Mountain and Road Circuits Aggregate Award, fairly easily, with 28 points with Reg second with 20, and Ian Connell third with 14. The situation was further complicated by the international situation for war now seemed almost a certainty despite Neville Chamberlain's assurance that we would 'Never go to war with Germany again.' So, feeling that the Bugatti had outlived its usefulness, I decided to try to find a buyer which I did — at no profit or loss to Bugatti fancier Cleveland Harmer.

Though he never actually said so, I got the impression from Carol Holbeach that Railton chief, Noel Macklin, was so convinced that war was imminent that car production had almost ceased and a search for war contracts had already begun. Much as I was enjoying car racing, I found that I was missing the bike side and, one day, when lunching with

Francis Beart, I asked him to let me know if he ever wanted a machine ridden. "No Charles, really? I thought that as the car side was going well for you, bikes were out. But how about riding the three fifty and sidecar on the 'Outer' at the July Meeting? So that was what I did.

It wasn't uneventful either. Such strange things happen in racing! I took the outfit out on the morning of July 14th, the day before the race, confident of how pleasant and enjoyable it would be only to find it most 'Un-Beart like' and a pig. Poor old Francis had my set up for the first two races; Johnny Lockett in the third, a five lap Mountain Race on a five hundred bored out to 502cc; Lockett again with a three fifty in Race 4, the 25 Lap Mountain Championship and again in Race 6, the Senior Mountain Championship. So, though he listened patiently to my moans of bad handling, that was all he could do till later in the afternoon. Meanwhile I tried to help myself by altering tyre pressures, fork springs and damper settings, all to no avail. So, after putting everything back where it was, I just had to

The Bugatti at Brooklands on the 11th of May 1939 when it won the 3rd Mountain Handicap. Racing motor-cyclist Adrian Earle at the starting handle, Roger Acland with the plug spanner and Bill Langrish (unpaid like the others) who maintained the car for 10 years. However all three had a 'bet on' with the Brooklands Bookie that day.

await the 'Maestro'. At four o'clock, an hour before the track closed, we got together. One look and: "Sod it. Sorry Charles. See if you can find a big block of wood, two or three big nails, and a hammer. A large hunk of railway sleeper would be best." Though I thought he'd gone mad, I found all three and took them over to his shed. Unzipping the tonneau of the sidecar, he jammed the block of wood in its nose, securing it to the floor with the nails. "So sorry about that. Forgot I'd removed the ballast. Try it now." And, of course, it handled perfectly.

Warm up, change plug for a 'hot' one, make for the Paddock exit gate to find Jack Cann, the gateman, just closing it for the day. Beat him to it with one finger held up

to denote 'one lap only'. He acknowledges it. Perfect handling down the railway straight, so much so that there's no problem taking it close in to the bottom of the Byfleet instead of lifting slightly at the entrance, to be on the safe side. Full bore all the way round, cut the engine to get a mixture reading, engine dead for the length of the finishing straight. Stop to thank Jack. The 'Maestro' is smiling.

He looks anxious. "Alright now?" "Spot on." "Good. Sorry about that. It's been a sod of a day. Bet you didn't think to 'chop' the engine at the fork?" "Of course I did." He removed the plug. "Good, that's all right. How early can you be here to practice in the morning?" "Any time you like. But I don't

need any more — unless you want me to."
"No, not if you're happy with it. Your rides
are in the first two races, at two thirty and
again at two fifty so, if you'd like to collect
the outfit between one thirty and two, put
it in its bay, I'll meet you there at two."

Saturday July 15th dawned dry and bright.
A quick run with the Speed Six, stop at the
'White Lion' at Cobham to find Charlie
Brackenbury and George Harvey Noble
there with some pints and some humour.
"What's all this about you riding a sidecar,
'Champ'? Dangerous things you know. Have
you ever ridden one before? Once a sidecar
wheel lifts on the Byfleet there's no getting
it back, you know — it's 'over the top' on
two wheels only. You'd be well advised to
take George or I as 'passenger and advisor'
"— and so on.

The meeting was 'Mountain Championship' Day with, as usual, quite a big gate.
Francis was well on time with a programme.
"Have a look at this, Charles and tell me
how you want to play it. Eighteen entries
in each race, all solos except ourselves." I
knew what I thought. "I leave it to you. We
could give it everything in both races. But
quite a few runners in the first race are in
the second one as well. Some may be
rehandicapped and set back a bit in the
second so I would have thought that Race
Two would be the better chance. But I don't
know if there's a real chance in either."

"I don't think there is for a win. But it
might get a place. Tell you what. Give it the
lot in both but do an easier standing lap in
the first and try for a real sparkling one in
the second. You might just scrape a place
that way."

We didn't really do our sums correctly in
retrospect. Francis' 'number one' rider,
Denis Minett, much smaller and lighter than
I, had just previously done an official
100mph lap on that particular machine and
since the fitting of a sidecar knocked at least
fifteen miles an hour off solo speed, we were
looking at a likely lap speed of around eighty
five. The limit man, Leveson Gower on an
ex-works 250cc Cotton to whom we were
handicapped to give fifteen seconds start in
three laps, looked well placed, always
assuming that none of the backmarkers had
surprises in stores — which, in fact, they
had! Reporting the two races, 'The Motor
Cycle' said "After one lap, Leveson Gower
led by the length of the Vickers straight from
C. K. Mortimer who it was good to see back
again in the saddle of F. L. Beart's 348cc
Norton and sidecar. With two laps covered,
it was obvious that Leveson Gower was
increasing his lead over Mortimer while G.
W. Field (496 Triumph) and L. A. Howe (497
Ariel) had separated from the pack and were
coming up fast enough to battle with
Mortimer for second place" — which in fact
they did rather successfully, relegating us to
fourth.

But on the start line for race two, Francis
was in good form. "Right. Better than we
thought. Both flying laps were excellent,
eighty six point six two and eighty seven
point three eight. The three fifty sidecar Lap
Record stands at eighty eight point three. See
what you can do, Charles. Have you got
anything left?" "Nothing on the throttle I'm
afraid. But I'll take it lower on both
bankings." "Not too low on the Home Banking. You'll lose time if it starts sliding. But
screw it really hard all the way."

Again The Motor Cycle — "For his
audacity, Leveson Gower was rehandicapped
in the second race and on the one minute,
six seconds mark was now giving twelve
seconds to Mortimer who jumped away
smartly at the start and held on to a good
lead for two laps and for the greater part of
the third. He looked like winning as he came
off the Byfleet banking alone but on the run
up to the finishing line, V. N. Hood, who
had been eighth at the beginning of the lap,
streaked past. About fifty yards past Mortimer
came R. Fazan (348 Velocette), O. E. de Lissa

(348 Norton) and J. M. Givons (348 Velocette)." Two quite interesting races for the fee-paying customers but, like all limit mark riding, dull to ride. But the 'Maestro' was happy. "Sparkling standing lap. Eighty seven point three eight second lap, eighty eight point one five third lap. Only just missed it! No one could say you didn't try. Look at this." As he spoke, he was pulling 'this' from the sidecar wheel and from beneath the chassis, a mass of compacted grass 'mown' from the verge at the bottom of the byfleet banking, not unusual where sidecars were concerned because, at any speed above the mid eighties and when taking the closest possible bottom line, the sidecar wheel never actually touched the ground for the whole three quarter mile distance of the banking but hovered as much as eight to ten inches off the ground, turning slowly and if collecting a lot of 'foliage' sometimes revolving backwards!

I'd been riding sidecars for some time before I discovered this Brooklands 'quirk', the discovery being made when following E. G. Bishop's three fifty Excelsior into the 'bottom' line during the 'tow' I was getting from him, I noticed his sidecar wheel lift and stay lifted all the way round. It made me wonder why, since we were on the same line, his 'chair' wheel lifted while mine didn't. The event was the 1934 Hutchinson 100 Mile Race so I had plenty of time to ponder over it before deciding to risk a quick look, and when I did, being rather shaken to find that I could count the number of spokes! The Beart Norton outfit handled so beautifully and imparted such confidence that, at the same time, it seemed reasonable to go just slightly more deeply into the 'undergrowth' but, with hindsight, it was probably lucky that there weren't any unchartered tree stumps there!

That foray led to something else because, by the time we lunched together next day, Francis had had a mull through the current list of World Records, and discovering that the 350cc Sidecar Standing Mile and Standing Kilo had stood for thirteen and nine years respectively was urging to attack them, and would I like to have a go? I said "Of course" but suggested a smaller and lighter rider but he'd already thought of that and knew of no one with experience of sidecars. So the attempt was planned for July 22nd, at Brooklands.

By this time war was the only topic of conversation and one knew that any plans one made would be liable to indefinite cancellation. I thought a lot about it before deciding that, if I could make it, the Navy or R.A.F. would be my choice but felt also that, while I would keep the single seater MG for the time being, I must go ahead and replace the Bugatti with something fast enought to be competitive in Scratch races, a task far from easy with only £50 in the bank plus £150 from the proceeds of the Bugatti sale.

So back again to the Brackenbury Advice Bureau. Charles was just back from Le Mans where he'd been driving one of the two V12 Lagondas partnered by Arthur Dobson while the second V12 had been driven by Lord Selsdon and Lord Waleran. The race had been highly successful for Lagondas, Charles' car finishing third behind the other car after a longish pit stop to fix a loose exhaust pipe. He had no doubt about the answer to my problem — it was "Talk to John about the twelve cylinder Sunbeam. He's asking £500 for it but there are no takers so far. He's a nice chap. He knows and likes you and has seen you ride several times. He was here, in fact, when you won the Mountain Championship." I knew John Cobb only slightly, through Charles, of course, who had partnered him on several occasions with the big Napier Railton and the 4 litre Sunbeam. Charles knew the Sunbeam well, having driven it, partnered by Powys Lybbe in the 1937 Five Hundred Miles Race when it finished fourth at 120 mph with a best lap of 132.8mph while John, partnered by Oliver Bertram won with the big Napier Railton at a record average of 127.8mph.

But how could one possibly go to buy a car priced at £500 with only £200 in one's pocket? Again, Charles had the answer "Look, you'll never get it if you don't try. He comes down to Thompson & Taylor's quite often. I'll talk to him and fix a meeting."

The meeting was fixed for July 22nd, the day that we were to have a shot at the three fifty sidecar records in the afternoon. Charles, John and Ken Taylor were there standing beside the car and after some opening conversation, John turned to me and said "Charles tells me you'd like to buy the Sunbeam." Ken, tactfully, left and I said "I would. But I really shouldn't be here because, as Charles knows, I just don't have that sort of money." John smiled and said "Well, take the car out and try it." Feeling sure that no deal was going to take place, I said "No, I won't do that but many thanks for the offer. I think I've seen the car in every Brooklands race it's run and Charles has told me all about it. I think that what I must do is to try and amass something nearer the price you want and then, if I may, talk to you again." "But you'd enjoy owning and driving it wouldn't you?" said John. "Of

The twelve cylinder Sunbeam when Sir Malcolm owned it leading Raymond Mays in the Invicta. The next owner John Cobb sold it to the author for £210.

The Sunbeam as it is now, valued at £1,000,000 and recently tested at over 150mph.

course. But it isn't fair to you to go any further at this stage." Apparently quite enjoying the conversation, John said "Well, would you like to tell me what sort of price you could offer for it at this moment?" I took a very deep breath and said "At this moment, I've got £210 in the bank. And, really, I need the £10 to get me through next week." There was a moment's pause and he said "Why not take an overdraft. An overdraft of £10 wouldn't cost you much." It took a moment to sink in. I said "I'm not sure what you mean. But I'd give all I've got right now." "Right then, that's a deal. The car is yours." I couldn't believe it.

Everyone had the highest regard for John but, even now, when his name crops up, my thoughts always go back to the Sunbeam. While researching this book I came across the handwritten receipt he gave me (reproduced here) and even though I paid him by cheque, he was still insistent that I ought to take the car out before leaving, that morning.

I went back to the paddock and found Francis and the Norton outfit ready and waiting. We'd envisaged an easy run and the whole thing taking about half an hour but in the end it took most of the afternoon, many runs and much hard work and bad language from Francis before we had the Standing Mile and Kilo records 'in the bag'. We just couldn't understand how the holders could possibly have done the speeds

The receipt for the £210 Charles Mortimer paid to John Cobb in 1939 for the Sunbeam. Approximately 0.02% of its 1990 value.

they did, all those years ago, with hand gear changes and with three speed gearboxes while we must have had more power helped by four speeds and foot change. The clutch became tired and had to be replaced and it was while this was being replaced that I had an idea. I was quite sure of one thing — that, during their runs, the oldsters must have had the throttle open all the time and never used the clutch when changing up — there was no other possible way they could have done it. On our Nortons we always withdrew clutches and shut off momentarily when changing up but when winning the 'Six fastest' event at Gatwick, I'd tried the 'full throttle no clutch' technique for the first and only time — and it had worked. The technique needed a hard stamp on the pedal to make sure of not missing the change — and wrecking the engine and was one that I felt sure Francis wouldn't accept. But I told him and was relieved when he didn't explode.

"Hmm. The snag to that is the first fifty yards. With a higher gear ratio, the clutch is going to take it all." Hearing the conversation the A.C.U. timekeeper, who had timed Marchant way back in 1926, came up with "Ah now, all this rings a bell. Dougal had all the problems you've got. He certainly didn't shut the throttle when changing gear — and when it came to the problem of clutch load off the line, he had the start line flooded with water to induce temporary wheelspin." So that was what we did with results —

	New Record Speed kph	Previous Record kph
Standing Kilometre	103.39	Holder. Melichar (Sunbeam) at, Hungary. October 1st, 1930
	103.39kph	100.33kph

74

Standing Mile	Holder. Dougal Marchant. (Chater Lea) at Appajon. France. September 5th, 1926.
113.47kph	110.73kph

Tired, not used to this sort of hassle, we were about to start the machine for the last time when the timekeeper came running from his box. "Wait a minute. You're doing the run both ways. Has the line at the other end been flooded?" It hadn't of course, so that meant further delay. But in the end it was alright.

Though I said nothing to Francis, there was a slight incident on this last return run. By that time, the engine had thrown out a lot of castor base which made the footgearchange pedal slippery and though the change from third to top went in alright, my foot slipped off the pedal and, with my weight on it, disappeared under the cradle of the frame. Instinctively I gave a mammoth heave to the left, conscious as I did it of a sharp pain in my stomach which, when I got off the outfit, was worse. Such things as hernias were unknown to me at the time but — yes, I had one — quite a bad one, the result being surgery — but not before I'd been up to the B.A.R.C. office to enter the Sunbeam for a Mountain Circuit race at the August Bank Holiday meeting on the 7th

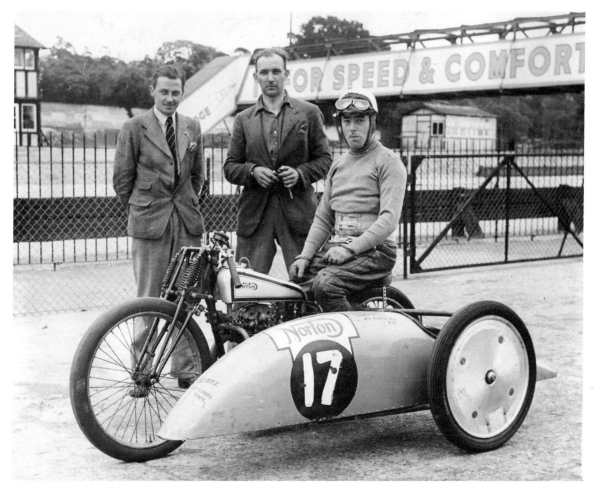

John Rowland, Francis Beart and Charles Mortimer before the attempt on the world's standing start mile and kilometre records. After 3 wrecked clutches they made it.

and — for good measure — the Magnette for one on the Road Circuit.

A call at the surgery of our family doctor produced not only the news of a hernia but that since it seemed to him to have complications, the operation would be better done in London and especially if he could procure the services of a surgeon called Mr. Ogier Ward. I tried to get out of this, by saying that all I needed was a quick repair to enable me to drive at Brooklands on Bank Holiday Monday — but got nowhere and was duly decanted, next day, at the portals of the Beuchens Nursing Home in Beaumont Street where, later in the day, I met Mr. Ogier Ward explaining my problem to him despite his apparent austerity. But despite my first impression of him, he turned out to be not only a marvellous surgeon but also a very human and nice man. After confirming the diagnosis, he listened to my problem and said "Alright, then, Let's make a deal. I won't impose a total ban for the 7th with two provisos, the first being that you can certainly drive if you truly feel that, on the day, you can do this very fast car justice. The second is that you agree to my advising, in writing, the Brooklands authorities the exact agreement that you and I have made."

Francis was my first visitor after the operation, blaming himself for what had happened — quite unfairly. Charles was the next, calling my attractive young nurse "a beautiful creature', asking her for a large Scotch since the sight of blood made him feel faint and finally being asked to leave when he made me laugh so much that one of the stitches tore. Jock Forbes was the next with the news that Railton were ceasing production and that Noel Macklin, after abortive visits to the War Office and Air Ministry in search of War contracts had finally procured one from the Admiralty and that Carol Holbeach had joined him as general manager and he, Jock had accepted the job of Transport Manager, his first task being to find an assistant which he hoped would be me. It was good of him but I'd always sheered away from office life and felt that that wasn't something I would be good at or wanted to do, grateful as I was for the offer. He said he quite understood what I felt but didn't seek an answer there and then but felt that war or no war, I'd be foolish to turn it down till I knew what it involved, adding that it was a new and exciting project being given absolute top priority, with many other contracts to follow if all went well.

I had the operation on July 24th and left the nursing home, accompanied by my anxious mother, our taxi being involved in a slow but quite forceful head-on collision on the way home, seeing the wisdom of Ogier Ward's words underlined within twenty four hours. With such a dark and menacing horizon my mother and I had both agreed to put our house on the market and a buyer had been quickly found in the form of a textiles company in the process of hurriedly evacuating their London offices to an area rather safer. I didn't feel ill in the least, just devoid of energy as I sat in the garden enjoying the sunshine. Contracts for the sale of the house had been exchanged and a completion date set but, understandably, the buyers were urging to get in before the axe fell and, to me, the whole thing seemed unreal. I'd wanted Charles to drive the Sunbeam for me but he'd said 'No' adding that if something had broken when he'd been driving it for John, it wouldn't have been a major disaster since John had better resources than he or I. I offered Jock West, an old bike racing friend and rival, the Magnette drive and he went well and enjoyed it.

The Programme of the Bank Holiday meeting arrived by post from Charles — very interesting because both he and Peter Selsdon were driving their Le Mans V12 Lagondas in the first Outer Ciruit Handicap which Charles won at 118.45mph with a best lap of 127.70, Peter finishing a good second. It was no surprise to find the Sunbeam on the Scratch mark in the First Mountain Handicap which it shared with Arthur Baron's 3.3 litre Type

59 G.P. Bugatti and Hyde's ex-Earl Howe 3 litre Maserati but it was rather surprising to find the Magnette also well set back on Scratch in the Third Road Handicap with Bob Gerards 1½ litre Riley sharing the same mark; it was no surprise to hear, later, that Bob had won. Non-starters were conspicuous by their absence; it was certainly the best supported meeting of 1939 and Charles came over to see me next day to bring me up to date though, at the time, we still didn't realise that it was to be the last ever and that we would be at war with Germany within a month.

There was certainly plenty to be done now. My mother had found a flat that she liked, facing the sea at Brighton, the home front was pretty hectic with Messrs Guthrie, the new owners already moving in and I had to get over to Brooklands to vacate my shed and clear everything out. I managed quite quickly to find a buyer for the Magnette; Robert Arbuthnot, with whom I had had previous dealings, phoned to say that he had a buyer for the Sunbeam but before deciding whether or not to sell it, I went over to see Ken Taylor to see if he would be willing to put it in mothballs and store it 'for the duration'.

His advice was brief and to the point — "Sell it." When I queried it he said "No, sell it. That car's got welded steel water jackets. This war is going to last five years, no matter how many people keep saying it'll be over by Christmas, and by then neither block will hold water." Rather against my own judgement, I took his advice and sold it to Mr. James, Robert's customer, and when I next saw the Sunbeam, at the first post war Brighton Speed Trials, driven by Jack Smith, it was losing water in all directions — there's no advice like an expert's.

While I was clearing out my shed, Francis came rushing round in a panic. "Quick, Charles. Have you got a rake, — or a fork — even a plank?" He grabbed a broom and was gone. Obvious drama, and how dramatic it was! The B.A.R.C. was having a grand office clearout and everything was being thrown on to a giant merrily blazing bonfire — and when one says everything, it really did seem to be everything: huge cardboard boxes containing hundreds of past unsold programmes, many others of documents, carpets, sacks full of B.A.R.C. car badges and even the big plaque mounted on the wall of the Clubhouse commemorating Percy Lambert's 'First 100 Miles in One Hour' run with the big Talbot, on February 15th, 1913 — the day that I was born. Grabbing my broom from Francis, I

The famous ex. Woolf Barnato 'Blue Train' Speed Six Bentley. Bought by the author in 1938 who sold it at the outbreak of war for £25 to replace it with a Ford Popular in order to save petrol. Like the Sunbeam which went at about the same time this car is now also valued at around £1,000,000.

rescued the plaque 'first go' and went to work stamping out the fire in the area of the badges while he continued to 'rake' furiously, in the end getting them all out undamaged as far as we could see but leaving the programmes partly on the basis of no value but also because their boxes were now blazing and blackened together with countless small boxes containing Members Lapel Badges. Though all the car badges were unharmed, we just might have salvaged more with water than with the broom!

Rolling the spoils in a tin wheelbarrow back to Francis' shed, we spread out and checked the spoils. I said 'D'you think we ought to check it with the office?'' and Francis said "Wouldn't have thought so. They dumped it and we saw who did it. But we can if you like." We did, to loud laughter and "What good is all that to anyone. Do what you like with it."

I wanted the plaque for obvious reasons, keeping it until the 1960's when, at the time of a house move, I gave it myself to Lord Montagu when the Beaulieu museum was beginning to get going well. I didn't see it again for a long time but I believe that it's now being exhibited. We divided the badges on a 75% Francis, 25% myself basis, later adjusted to 80%-20% because I felt that one day the plaque would be worth more. What, I wonder, would it all be worth today? Yes, I think so too.

But, for me that wasn't the end of Brooklands. I learned from Jock that the Admiralty contract Noel Macklin had procured was for the construction of a 110-foot, timber-built multi-purpose boat, prefabricated and to be built at the yards of small boatbuilders all round the coast of England, Scotland and Wales who had the facilities and capacity to undertake the work and that, at the moment Carol Holbeach was in the process of touring the coasts in search of possible builders and was expected back within the next week. At that time, he and Jock totalled the adminis-trative side and while Jock, as Transport Manager, would be responsible for transport policy and administration, there was a place for me as assistant, responsible more for the operative side which, though it would obviously involve some office work would require at least as much time spent away from and outside the office. Between 100 and 150 road vehicles would be involved, ranging from 5 cwt vans to diesel lorries with a 15 ton carrying capacity, while, later, some material would go by rail.

Components for the boat would come in from sub-contractors to a number of scattered warehouses and be issued to the various builders as and when needed and the larger timber items would be constructed and issued from one big timber mill on the outskirts of London, the keel of a boat going out first, then frames and bulkheads and finally planking and joinery. It did sound rather interesting — and I could have a week to think about it.

And Brooklands? Well, at the outbreak of war there was so much to think about, so much to be done and so many decisions to take that there was no time to think about Brooklands which, with its aircraft side, seemed to be looking after itself. But by the mid 1940's its post-war future could have been and should have been thought about and, apart from the vendors themselves, the blame for its demise, I think, lies fairly and squarely on my generation. Whether or not the track could or couldn't have been a viable motoring or motor racing proposition, I'm not qualified to say, but when I see the wonderful work that the Brookland Society has done, the results it has achieved, the crowds that derive such enormous pleasure with their beautifully restored and maintained cars, increasing in number and quality at each successive re-union, I feel amost ashamed to be welcomed as a guest because I and my generation certainly played a part in letting this later generation down. Every time I go to the re-union, I feel increasingly how wonderful it would be if a programme like the one of August 7th, 1939, and others equally good, could be staged today. I do think, despite the fact that I missed it, that last programme exceeded all others in variety of interest, consisting of:

Race 1. Campbell Circuit. 5 Laps. Handicap. 12 Entries included ERA's, Bugatti, Monoposto, Alfa Romeo, Maserati & MG's.

Race 2. Campbell Circuit. 5 Laps. Handicap. Similar plus BHW, Alta, Delahaye etc.

Race 3. Campbell Circuit. 5 Laps. Handicap. Similar, plus Alvis, Riley, Frazer Nash etc.

Race 4. Campbell Circuit. Campbell Trophy. 10 Laps. scratch, 3 Alfa Romeos plus Maserati, Alta & Multi Union & 6 ERA's.

Race 5. Special Circuit. 2 Laps. Handicap. Cars manufactured pre 1901. 25 Entries. Scratch car 1901. Limit car 1896.

Race 6. Special Circuit. 2 Laps. Handicap. Cars 1902 to 1904. 25 Entries.

Special Event. Outer Circuit. Demonstration by Maj. A. T. G. Gardner of his 200mph. record breaking MG.

Race 7. Mountain Circuit. 5 Laps. Handicap. 15 Entries included Alta, Bentley, Bugatti, Maserati, MG, Riley, Darracq & Sunbeam

Race 8. Mountain Circuit. 5 Laps. 14 Entries included Appleton Special, 4 ERA's, Aston Martin, Harker Special & Multi Union.

Race 9. Mountain Circuit. 5 Laps. Handicap. 14 Entries plus BHW & Delahaye.

Race 10.. Outer Circuit. 3 Laps. Handicap. Alvis, Bentley, Bentley Jackson, Lagonda, Graham Paige & Amilcar.

Race 11. Outer Circuit. 3 Laps. Similar plus Alfa Romeo & Duesenberg.

Race 12. Outer Circuit. 5 Laps. Handicap. Alta, Alvis, Aston Martin.

Frazer Nash, Frazer Nash-BMW, Talbot etc.

Special Event. Attempt on John Cobb's Outer Circuit Lap Record of 143.44mph with the Napier Railton by C. S. Staniland (Multi Union).

We have the cars today, we have the drivers. For every race meeting held pre-war in the U.K. a dozen must be held today — and

Brooklands could have had other uses. A shame we let it die competitively though, thanks to its present owners and the Brooklands Society great that we can, now and then, get a glimpse of it.

Though I hadn't expected it, I was quite quickly advised by the B.A.R.C. that, with thirty eight points, I had been adjudged winner of the Campbell and Mountain circuits Aggregate Award with Reg Parnell runner up with twenty eight and Peter Aitken third with twenty five; a result which in the circumstances and bearing in mind that the total sum invested in the Bugatti and Magnette only totalled £400 was quite pleasing.

Our house move, from rather a large house in which we had been for twelve years, to a lovely but smaller flat, was a nightmare, with much having to be put into store. While mulling over Jock's now rather interesting proposition, I saw quite a lot of George Harvey Noble and Charlie Martin, both Brighton residents. After a visit to Cobham to see Jock and meet Carol and also Noel Macklin, I accepted the invitation happily, provided I could be given another three weeks before actually starting with the Fairmile Marine Company, so as to help my mother settle into the flat and make my own plans for moving back again to the Weybridge area.

That left only GJ3811 the Barnato Bentley Speed Six Coupe to be dealt with; though, at the time, there was literally no market for a car of its size and type, the future was so uncertain that it had to go despite the fact that, for some time, it proved impossible to find a buyer for it at any price.

Then, on the day of the 'Brooklands Bonfire', who should walk in but 'Woolley' Worters, fresh from his triumphant building of Chris Stanilands' Alfa Romeo engined Multi Union, the second fastest car ever to go round Brooklands at only about a mile an hour slower than John Cobb's 143mph lap record. He was rightly cross with Chris for their failure to take the record at that last meeting on

August 7th. Woolley's version of the story behind it was that his mandate had been to prepare the car for an attempt on the record which he agreed to, provided that the car didn't run in any races that day prior to the record attempt. So setting the car up for the Lap Record attempt only, he was annoyed to find it down to run in two earlier Outer Circuit races, two five lap Mountain races and the ten lapper for the Campbell Trophy. Chris was a superb driver but tended to be hard on the car so that when, at the end of the day, the Lap Record attempt was made, the engine was in no fit state for record breaking of any sort even though it lapped at 142.30 with a holed piston and on seven cylinders in the attempt and had been timed in one of its previous races at 160mph down the Railway straight. I said I knew how he must feel — but that was Chris. "Yes, that's it. If he wasn't such a super chap one would have nothing to do with him. But he threw that record away just as though he'd thrown the clutch out on full throttle during the attempt. The car would have lapped at 145mph if he hadn't thrashed it in those races previously — all for nothing.

He looked across at the Bentley gloomily. "What are you doing with that, keeping it or selling it?" I said that, with enormous regret, I wanted offers for it. "How would you feel about £20?" I felt I'd take it but must try for more. "I'd rather keep it. I'd let it go for £35 though." "£22 then?" He obviously did want it and had to be taken seriously. If he didn't have it, Lord only knew what would happen to it. "Look Woolley, as it's you, I'll let it go for £25. Don't bid me again. That's it." He wrote out the cheque and it was with real sadness that I saw him drive off. There were just too many complications to do it any other way.

That, then, was Brooklands. But not quite, because these notes have made no mention of 'Ebby'. A. V. ('Ebby') Ebblewhite, Brooklands Timekeeper and Handicapper from when the track opened in 1907 to the time it closed in 1939, should really have written a book of his own. Regarded by both riders and drivers as very much the schoolmaster, he did a magnificent job always. All the timekeepers were regarded by the riders, to some extent, mainly figures of fun because whereas we were young and fun loving, they were elderly and serious. Generally, they did a difficult job, in difficult circumstances and, probably, with equipment far less good than it became later. They were almost over-conscious of their authority and their decisions were almost never questioned. But from time to time they inevitably made mistakes. I always used to check all our lap times with 'Ebby' by post after each meeting and on one occasion, a five lap outer circuit race with a big Norton, received from him 'Standing Lap, 95mph, Flying, 105, 104, 105 and 109mph. I had to query it, knowing that the last lap couldn't possibly have been done at a hundred and nine and that if it wasn't queried, we should be handicapped to lap at a hundred and nine next time out, and from then on. Trying to spare his blushes, I wrote saying that the error could well have come about due to the fact that our race number wasn't clearly painted as it might have been, and apologising, even though the number was just as clear as it had been on our other bikes that day. Back came a letter, correcting the error and adding "You are quite right. Your number was very indistinctly painted and caused considerable confusion in the timing box. Please make sure that this doesn't happen again." But on another occasion when, by mistake, I went up to the start with no number at all, they couldn't have been nicer about it!

The funniest thing I ever saw was on yet another occasion. As I was passing the front of the timing box, 'Ebby's' head popped out of the window with "Mortimer. You don't seem to be doing anything. We're a man short up here. Come up and give us a hand." It was a five lap outer circuit race again, this time with a very big field and a superb bit of handicapping on his part because, for once,

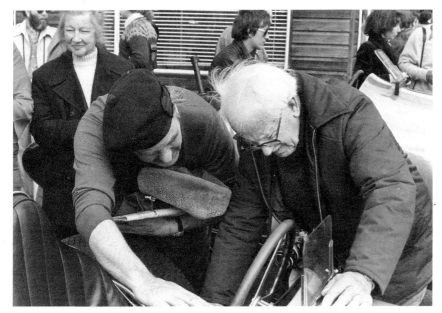

In 1939 J.S. 'Woolley' Worters transformed Chris Staniland's 'Monoposto' Alfa Romeo into the Multi Union which lapped Brooklands at 142 mph. — — fifty years later Charles Mortimer (right) introduced 'Woolley' (centre) to the then owner The Hon Patrick Lindsay at a Brooklands re-union meeting.

the first five finishers crossed the line as one — quite magnificent. But once the others had come in and returned to the paddock, there was deadly silence in the box. I realised what an awful situation existed, because, not only as timekeepers but also as judges, no-one in the box had the remotest idea of who had won, and worse still, there was an outsider in the box with them, so the matter certainly couldn't be discussed. Moments passed with everyone gazing down at their sheets before, in clarion tones, 'Ebby' pronounced not only the first, second and third men to finish but also the winner's speed to three, instead of the usual two, decimal points! I recall asking if I was needed for the next race and being told "No, no. Many thanks we're alright now " and watching, with other riders afterwards, the tremendous discussion that went on in the box after my departure!

But I think that, though I wasn't there to see it, the funniest timekeeping situation of all must have been the one on the occasion of the first Double Twelve Hour Race at the track in the early thirties. One race run over two twelve-hour days required the fullest possible complement of timekeepers and a number long since 'put out to grass' were co-opted, including one very old one who arrived in a bowler hat and a raincoat. Even in those days, bowlers had long been out of fashion at Brooklands and this one was the cause of much merriment, so much so that Charlie Brackenbury and Chris Staniland decided to make the most of it. Once the first practice day had started, they crept into the timing box, removed the hat from its peg and measuring it and finding not only its size but also that it was brand new and supplied by Bentalls of Kingston, replaced it and left hotfoot to Kingston where they bought two identical hats — one two sizes smaller, the other two sizes larger. Back at Brooklands they again entered the timing box, just before the lunch break, replacing the original with the much smaller one. Ready for a break after his morning's work, the owner put on the hat and, finding it perching on top of his head, looked in vain for another. Not finding one, he left with it under his arm and returned later still carrying it. Looking concerned, he again searched the line of pegs, finally replacing it to do his after-noon stint. Once that had started, the ultra-small hat was replaced with the ultra-large one which, at the end of the day, fell down over the victims ears so that once more he left carrying it. Next morning — day two of the practice — he didn't turn up and when 'phoned by the Club, his wife answered with, "I'm so glad you've called. I was going to 'phone you anyway. My husband's not well at all. We're waiting for the doctor now. My husband's been sitting in his armchair all night, measuring his head hourly with a tape measure."

But the panel of Brooklands timekeepers were great men, and in retrospect, the part that 'Ebby' played was enormous, for it was he who first devised the handicapping system which, though it may at first have been fairly obvious and simple when only the Outer circuit was used, must have become more and more complicated when first the Mountain circuit, and later the Campbell circuit, were added. And, of course, the Test Hill and World Record attempts both required timekeepers. But we, the runners, took it all for granted, just as we had Brooklands itself.

My ten years spent in racing bikes and cars at Brooklands were the most carefree of my life. Like W. O. Bentley and others I shunned the idea of a 'Nine to Five' office job though, from the point of view of finance it would have been wiser to have opted for one. But the people I met, the cars and bikes I enjoyed owning, driving and racing have left memories that could never be erased. And, of course, though the personalities are thinning out, I still enjoy seeing the cars being even better driven at Silverstone in the hands of their new owners and since we now live only ten miles from the circuit, I try never to miss a Grand Prix or a V.S.C.C. Meeting there. Even nicer is the fact the British Racing Driver's Club has now generously made antiquities like me Life Members which means that we can do it all in the greatest comfort.

In retrospect it has interested me to see how one phase of my life has led to another so that, in turn, I've been, first, a dealer and competitor, then a transport man, back to competitor, once again to dealer, from there to motoring bookdealer and finally a dealer in motoring art in the form of motoring mascots, badges, trophies and memorabilia which I now enjoy almost most of all while, from time to time varying the diet by becoming author. I don't mind the 'evening of life' at all in its present form!

. . . the Start of a New One

I suppose that, today, Captain Noel Macklin would be dubbed with that dreadful description 'entrepreneur' for despite all his outstanding qualities he was primarily a man of ideas. But, more than that, during the five years I knew him he was essentially an inspiring leader, enthusiastic about what he was doing, untiring, a despiser of red tape and a man with whom it was a privilege to work. At that time, he was best known as manufacturer of the Invicta and, later, the Railton marques, though he had at least one earlier venture into motor manufacture. Time had been unkind to him where both the Invicta and the Railton were concerned; the Invicta, brilliantly conceived, elegant to a degree and exuding quality, was killed by the early 1930's recession and the Railton, an ingenious concept if ever there was one, suffered a similar fate due to the outbreak of war.

But Macklin had another quality. He was a fighter who would never take 'no' for an answer and it was no surprise to those who knew him to find him now, in 1939, the head of the Fairmile Marine Company. He had, for some time, seen the war was inevitable, envisaged the end of motor manufacture and, long before the crash came, had brushed off 'nos' from the Admiralty so, when the axe fell, he was well 'ahead of the ball.' Such a talented man could never have been stopped for long and his talents, of course, were inherited by his family: his son, Lance, became one of Britain's leading racing drivers after the war

and his wife, Lesley was one of three sisters, two of whom, Violet and Evelyn, had made history driving Invictas in the late 1920's and early '30's.

Though Noel had presence and a great aura of authority his leadership sprung essentially from inspiration and enthusiasm. Of medium height, always dapper and immaculate, he could, from time to time, get one off balance and I recall one occasion when he did this to me. Going through the entrance hall I found a man unattended and obviously needing attention. Noting his name and that he wanted to see the Chief, I went up to his office, knocked and told him. "Oh, that chap. Can't stand him. Tell him I'm out, would you. No, better still, tell him I'm in Scotland and won't be back for some time." I did so but the visitor was pressing and while we talked, Noel decided that, after all, he would see the chap and came scuttling down the stairs, full of enthusiasm and bonhomie. "Hello old chap. How nice to see you, come on up. Come on," leaving me feeling just a bit small.

The two things Noel impressed on all who worked for him at that time were first to have an air of hustle and secondly never to take 'no' for an answer, particularly if the 'no' came from someone in authority. Always counter the answer 'no' with the question 'why not' and go on saying 'why not' until success was attained; otherwise take it to a higher authority in the company who would keep doing the same till it reached him. And never, in any circumstances, accept 'because it's against regulations' as a refusal to do something. There had to be regulations, of course, but few couldn't be broken were the need to break them sufficiently great.

By the time I joined the company the initial contract for ten boats, designated 'A' class, was so well under way that two were already undergoing Amiralty trials with two more almost ready for builders trials; all well ahead of schedule, apparently instilling such confidence in the powers that be that a second contract for several hundred 'B' class boats followed shortly afterwards. Yards all round the coast as far apart as Littlehampton, Chichester, Southampton, Cowes, Poole, Plymouth, Falmouth, Looe, Par, Appledore, Bangor, Tarbert, St. Monance, Grimsby and Lowestoft were all working feverishly, with other yards being added almost weekly, with visits from progress chasers clearing supply bottlenecks at breakneck pace. The keynote was hustle and one automatically picked up the pace from the obvious enthusiasm of it all. The number one priority was that no builder should, even for a moment, be held up for an essential part or parts. The organisation was subdivided into teams for design, manufacture by sub-contractors, delivery to the company's stores at Hudson Motors at Chiswick and at Brooklands of all parts other than timber, and re-issue from the stores to each builder at the right time and in the right sequence — it was a prime example of prefabrication just beginning at that time. First to go out, from the timber mill at Brentford, was the keel of the boat and its frames and bulkheads, all on one big, rigid 15-ton eight-wheeled ERF or Foden, followed by load number two, planking and deck timbers. From then on the loads became smaller, being delivered by ten, five- and three-ton ridged vehicles, load number three being the two large Vee-12 Hall Scott petrol engines, each insured for £5000 in transit.

Initially, my plan had been to settle in to a small pub but since Jock or I or both of us had to be on call twenty four hours a day, with so many vehicles roaming the country and with a bedside phone essential, I finally had to settle for the Oatlands Park hotel at Weybridge, a rather grand place with a lake and situated in many acres of its own. For some reason that I never knew, 'O P H' was unlicensed though, acknowledging that guests did, from time to time, like a drink, all who did were routed to the 'Locker Room' where one was allocated a small locker in which to store one's drink. For all the grandeur of the hotel itself, the room hardly amounted to more than a very large cupboard! Packed to bursting capacity between the hours of seven and eight each evening, the Locker Room became a haven at the end of each day and one of my first meetings there was with Sir Thomas Bowen whose brother, Sir John, had been killed in a car racing accident at Donington.

Tommy and I used to enjoy drinks together pretty regularly in the Locker Room often discussing cars and motor racing but while, at that time, I was lacking a young lady, he seemed to know dozens. Among them was Jean Summers, older daughter of Captain and Mrs. Joseph Summers. I knew Summers' name from the Brooklands era because during all the time I'd been at Brooklands, he had been Chief Test Pilot for Vickers, the first man ever to take a Spitfire aircraft off the ground and at that time he was battling with the flight problems of things like Vickers Wellingtons and Warwicks. Though Jean appeared to be Tommy's 'Number One', she and I seemed to spend a lot of time together mainly because for all his excellent qualities, Tom wasn't the most punctual of men: so I don't think it surprised anyone when her allegiance veered from Tom to me.

The big difference between our office, staffed by Jock, his wife Violet and myself, and the rest of the Fairmile administrative side was that while the rest of the office hummed from Monday morning till Saturday night, ours being transport couldn't, for with around a hundred lorries out on the roads seven days a week there had to be a central point at which any driver with problems could phone, not only during the daytime but also, if necessary, at night. Initially Jock and I did alternative Sundays on a rota basis and night calls, when they came, as well. Technically, Violet was secretary to both of us which was great because I had known her as well as I knew Jock from the Brooklands days and she, too, soon became very transport-minded and took on much work really outside her allotted scope. Even at that early stage, in the early 1940's there wasn't much time for socialising and once the boats went into service, calls from Naval dockyards and bases requesting spares urgently, as well as calls from the builders, decreed that free time would be even less. So, by the the middle of 1940, socialising was limited to the Locker Room, an occasional pub 'dine out', or a visit to the movies. But it worked, and, in the end, the three of us kept it working right through to the end.

So many strange things happened. We had no less than five haulage fleets on permanent contract; Cliffords of Brentford, Adams Brothers of New Malden, Ballards of Twickenham and Steve Eastmeads in North London. Oh, and one more, S. Gwilt of Southampton, in some ways the best of all despite operating only one vehicle, a three-ton box van. Gwilt's proprietor was Gurney Smeed, an extrovert character who turned up out of the blue in search of work for his one-man business with the information that, as the black sheep of the family he had been given a lump sum to keep out of the way for the duration — and had we any work for him and his van? As it turned out, he couldn't have turned up at a better moment for one of the current transport problems was that the 'B'

class boat had a funnel which, till then, had consistently suffered damage in transit when loaded with other material. Measuring Gurney's magnificent 'Reo Speed Wagon' van, we found that it would just take not one but three funnels at a time and from then on he did nothing else but deliver funnels. Till then a big diesel had taken a week to deliver to and return from one of the Scottish builders but on his first trip — to Scotland — Gurney did it in two days, not altogether surprising because, apart from the fact that the cab was as luxurious as the most expensive of cars, it also had a maximum speed of 75 miles an hour, unloaded or loaded with funnels.

Throughout the war we had him on permanent contract and he not only did wonderful work but gave us many laughs. One of his contentions was that if any delivery went wrong, little could be done about it because since Mr. Gwilt had died long before he bought the business only he, Gurney, or the driver could take the blame and since he, Mr. Smeed, was never in the office and the driver, Mr. Smeed, was always on the road, there was only the long-deceased Mr. Gwilt to complain to! Later, when food rationing became stringent, he added a rifle with telescopic sights to the van's equipment, especially when on Scottish runs, steadfastly maintaining that he never shot a pheasant, grouse, partridge or hare unless it was actually on the road and in his way! He never at any time put in applications for lodging or food expenses, maintaining either that the yards to whom he delivered or the skipper of the boat whose spares he carried had lodged, fed and wined him.

Rather later, I was wakened at three o'clock one morning with a 'phone call from the night porter downstairs to say that two gentlemen were there and wanted to see me urgently. Wondering who they could possibly be, I dressed hurriedly to the accompaniment of teeming rain and a category one air raid. Outside in the drive, two huge eight-wheelers, laden to the sky, clanked away noisily. As I approached, one of their drivers, whom I knew, descended from his cab. I recognised him and both vehicles being under contract to the company though their loads obviously weren't our material. His reason for being there was unusual and unwelcome. They'd left Lowestoft with a load of Fairmile material early that morning. Returning to their yard in the evening they'd been met with a posse of Army brass who, on Government authority had impressed both vehicles and their drivers, instructing them to proceed immediately to Woolwich Arsenal where they would be re-loaded and given further instructions.

According to the driver the Government had been given a 'tip off' that there was to be an air raid on the Arsenal that night. Each vehicle was quickly loaded with twenty tons of gunpowder and told to pull out quickly to let other waiting lorries come in. Finding it impossible to get any delivery instructions they had thought it best to visit me! That seemed rather a liberty despite the circumstances but the first priority seemed to be to get both the vehicles as far away as possible from civilisation so, telling them to follow me, I hopped into my faithful wartime Ford Anglia and led the cortège to Wisley Common where, after locking the cabs, we left hurriedly en route to the drivers' homes in London. As soon as it was light I returned to the Common to find both vehicles intact and waited at what seemed a safe distance till the drivers returned in a mate's car. The air raid having blown itself out, they returned happily to their yard at Brentford to await further instructions!

As time passed it became obvious that Fairmile boats in service were to receive priority over boats in process of building. This applied particularly to the 'B' class boats which were 112 feet at the waterline, of round-bilge design and performing a variety of tasks including minelaying, harbour launch and Air-Sea Rescue. Funnels apart, the most difficult

things to transport were prop shafts which were thirty-two feet long and had to be supported for twenty feet of their total length on a flat platform. There was no problem about this apart from cost, which was now being increasingly taken into account. A year previously no one would have batted an eyelid at the thought of loading a couple of shafts weighing half a ton each on a six-wheeler capable of carrying fifteen tons — but now it was different: expense must be taken into account in addition to urgency. So when we had an urgent call one night four shafts to be sent A.S.A.P. to Scotland for two boats damaged in service, we had a problem in having no other load due to go up there.

We discussed it and presently Jock said "I wonder if we could send them on the Midnight Royal Scot leaving from Euston?" I said "Your're not serious?" and he replied "No, really. With a bit of help from the Admiralty Rail Transport Officer at Euston we might be able to thread them into the leading coach." So we 'phoned the R.T.O. who turned out to be young and full of zest. Explaining that while some carriages had corridors down the middle and straight, others, with 'loos' were at the side and were cranked at each end, adding that he'd have a look at the problem and call back within ten minutes. Good as his word, he came back with "Right, I think we might win this one. The leading coach corridor is straight and central for the length of the vehicle. The operation will be about as much against railway regulations as it can be — but that's my worry, not yours. But it's really important to have the shafts loaded before the locomotive backs down at 11.45. I can devise transport for the shafts from unloading your vehicle, down the platform to the train. But can you be at Euston with the load by eleven p.m. at the latest."

We were, and there he was with six four wheeled porters trolleys coupled as a train and four porters as power. Unloading and reloading wasn't easy and it was lucky that, at that stage, we were ahead of time. But at last it was done and we sprinted through the station and down to the end of the platform to find not one but two engines, with the buffers of the rear one's tender touching those of the leading coach but not actually coupled. We were met by a covey of officials, presided over by the stationmaster who informed us that what we proposed doing would, at any time, have been impossible but now was not even to be considered. The young R.T.O. who, it later turned out had been in action and wounded himself, now went into action in true 'Macklin' style, persuasive at first veering to become insistent, slightly threatening and, in the end, verging on blackmail. He frightened the posse so much that, with five minutes to go, both locomotives drew forward, the shafts were loaded and the train left only one minute late — it was magnificent.

Every day there were problems, increasingly difficult as the war went on. But every problem was different from the previous one and we always had the support of Carol Holbeach, General Manager, Mr. Cushman who was the Chief's right-hand man and, if necessary, the Chief himself. I may say 'Mr. Cushman' because, though I worked with him for nearly five years, Macklin and everyone else calling him 'Cushy' and I never knew him by any other name. Originally with Archie Frazer Nash and Dan Godfrey in the G.N. days, he was with Noel Macklin from the early Invicta era right to the end.

The faster the wheels turned, the heavier the load on the small Fairmile transport department became. Several lorries actually belonging to the company were drafted in and a small fleet of motorcycle despatch riders, mounted on side-valve Nortons, were added to maintain quick communication between the stores, the timber mill and head office. We became responsible not only for their running but also for their maintenance, which became such a headache that the maintenance was sub-contracted to Brooklands habitué John Rowland, who was running on his own a small garage in Byfleet.

By mid-1944 Jean and I had been 'going steady' for more than three years and I think it must have been around that time that the pressures began to ease and one began to think once more of cars, and motoring. My faithful 1939 Ford Anglia which had only two thousand miles on the clock when I bought it, came to a strange and sudden end at a mileage of over a hundred thousand when, one day, returning from Chiswick to Head Office at Cobham, I came up behind a convoy of Churchill tanks proceeding at around fifteen miles an hour under their own power. Traffic was coming the other way and it was impossible to get past so I latched on behind the tail ender. Suddenly the leader came to a halt so quickly that each one following had to stop more quickly still with the result that the old 'popular', almost brakeless from lack of maintenance, charged it with such force that it disintegrated in a cloud of rust and dust as completely as any car could. Without even noticing the impact the tank proceeded, its crew blissfully unaware of the incident, let alone the sad little corpse lying in the road behind them!

Offered a day off to buy new transport and with more money in my pocket than I had ever had, since at that stage of the war there was nothing to spend it on, I took train to London and made my way straight to Warren Street, the home of secondhand car trading. I spent most of the day there. My first buy was essential transport in the form of a mint 1939 Vauxhall 'Ten' Sports two-door coupe with a guaranteed mileage of ten thousand and documentation to prove it. It was great to be back in an atomsphere of motor trading for a few hours and I also bought a beautiful SS 100 Jaguar sports two seater with 3½ litre engine and quite a scarce car, a 2.6 litre MG four-door saloon, both fairly low mileage 1939 cars. The Vauxhall gave me completely trouble-free service for the rest of the war period and when the time came for its departure, I was sorry to see it go. I also made an exciting buy — a pristine pointed-tail MG Supercharged 'K3', a most unlikely car to find in Warren Street.

There'd been no exciting road motoring for years, of course. Or almost none, for Charlie Brackenbury, who'd taken over Eric Fernihough's garage on the Brooklands Road at Weybridge, had bought from Lagondas, just after the war started, the chassis — minus body — of the Vee-12 Lagonda that he'd driven so well with Arthur Dobson at Le Mans in 1939. It was agreed by the vendors of the MG saloon and SS100 two seater that those cars would be delivered to a three car lock-up garage that I rented in Weybridge but storage for the 'K3' presented a bit of a problem though; in the end, my mother found a small lock up down in Brighton. Charles, too, rose to the occasion, taking me up to town very early one Sunday morning in (or on?) the Lagonda Chassis to collect the 'K3'. Though both cars were on trade plates we decided not to tempt providence, driving both but leaving the Lagonda at Redhill and continuing together in the MG to Brighton. After lunching with my mother, we took the train back to Redhill continuing home from there on the chassis. Very much a day to remember!

By early 1945 there were signs of things beginning to return to normal. One was meeting and getting news of Brooklands drivers and though there was no basic petrol, one or two people were starting to give parties despite the shortage of such basic necessities as whisky or gin. So, with Jean's help, we set to and redecorated the lock up housing the SS and MG and held a party for old friends, even though all we

could find to drink was a barrel of beer! A week before the date, I was offered Hugh Hunter's single-seater blown Alta which I bought and which added atmosphere and, to increase it, we pinned on the walls my collection of Brooklands photographs. And despite the fact that nearly all the guests came by train and were met by taxi at Weybridge station and taken back afterwards, the 'do' was a howling success.

All through the war, the Fairmile company had been getting fresh contracts one after another, one being for a small number of 'C' boats, about which no one seemed to know much, followed by one for what were described as 'storage tanks' which were huge rectangular metal tanks, assumed to be for fuel storage for use in the invasion but which turned out to be sections of the invasion's 'Mulberry Harbour'; another, much more exciting and much larger, was for a run of 'D' boats, hard chine and much faster and more aggressive than the 'B's and powered by four V-12 Packards, much more powerful than the old Hall Scotts. From time to time members of the company were taken on trials on the boats, the object being to boost morale. When our turn came, Jock and I delayed it in order to take it on a Packard-powered 'D', which we did from Osborne's yard at Littlehampton, with Violet holding the fort in the office, the delay proving well worthwhile;

Not long after that, Noel Macklin was awarded a well deserved knighthood for his work throughout the war which he celebrated by giving an absolutely marvellous party at Head Office, emphasising in his speech that without the support he'd had the results could never have been achieved — but not mentioning his leadership. What was even more interesting was the point that he made underlining the fact that it wasn't only big companies that had made big contributions to the war effort and that the Admiralty had expressly emphasised this in the case of Fairmile. Everyone present became happily drunk and all drove home contentedly on almost deserted roads.

One last recollection. Many Fairmile boats took part in the invasion and, so as to conserve fuel, were towed across to France by freighters, six or eight at a time. This involved strengthening the fore and after decks with thick metal plates to which bollards were attached, the plates being described for security reasons at 'band-stands'. In our department we did know what these were but few did in other departments and when, one day, an enquirer sought from Jock the need for 'bandstands' he replied "Well, it's a question of morale really. Think of yourself making your way across the Channel to invade France. You'd be much happier with a Band of the Marines playing 'Land of Hope and Glory' on the foredeck than in dead silence, wouldn't you?" Happy to get this inside information, the recipient then broadcast it all round the office before being warned, for the sake of security, not to repeat it to the world at large.

The Clouds Roll By

After some months spent 'clearing up' at Fairmile, Jock and Violet left to visit his family in America and I found myself once more a dealer. Initially I planned to trade in a small way from my three-car Weybridge lock-up but when John Rowland told me that he was thinking of giving up the lease of his much larger garage in Byfleet I bought it, bringing the SS100, MG 2.6 and the Hunter Alta down as first items of stock but keeping the Vauxhall because of the petrol shortage. Initially, John managed the business but that didn't work well and in the end, he left and was replaced. I also bought a smaller freehold garage in Byfleet with a showroom to hold about a dozen cars and a flat above into which, at the time, I planned to move.

Charles said that Lagondas were keen to get back to racing and aimed to do Le Mans again and that they had offered him a position as their number one driver and asked him to suggest number two and that he had made the choice: me. He still had the pre-war chassis and said that they wanted to put a body on that and would like me to run a Lagonda Vee-12 saloon which I had bought on very favourable terms. But for a long time there weren't any races and the scene restarted appallingly slowly.

The very first post-war event was a rally staged by the M.C.C. in June 1945, not in the least like today's heart-stopping rallies but just a sort of 'get together' where old friends could meet and admire each others cars while swopping wartime experiences.

Much heralded by the motoring press, it was held at Wrotham Park and attracted a good entry including W.M. (Mike) Coupers Light 15 Citroen, Dorothy Patten's sports two-seater Peugeot Type 402, a rare car and one which was later to have sad memories for us, Leslie Johnson's Frazer-Nash-BMW Type 320 Coupe, Biggs' Allard, many Rileys and MGs, the odd Rover, our Lagonda and several Rolls'. There was nothing competitive about it but there must have been at least fifty nine cars, the weather was ideal and it was nice to just picnic and chat in the sunshine and admire the cars.

The next event, held a month later, was much more adventurous. Though still titled a rally and planned by Rivers Fletcher, it was officially an untimed parade of racing cars and super sports machinery, along a building site road to a roundabout, away from it down another road where one turned round and did the whole course the reverse way. Entrants included two ERAs, Bugatti Types 51 and 57, a vintage and historic G.P. Ballot, Sunbeam and Mercedes, a 38/250hp Mercedes, John Bolster's 'Bloody Mary', several other 'Specials', a Le Mans HRG and Peugeots. Like many others, we couldn't overcome the problems of transport to and from the venue at Cockfosters or the problem of obtaining racing fuel so took part in a car from stock, a really lovley 2.3 litre supercharged two-seater Castagna-bodied Alfa Romeo which, sporting a 'Monza' radiator cowl, wasn't at all out of character. Since we had now been married, Jean came with me as passenger.

Also well publicised by the press, the event sticks in one's mind for the massive entry; the fact that, to all intents and purposes it did become competitive even though untimed; and the enormous crowd of spectators it drew who lined not only the roads but also the roundabout itself, ten or more deep and with no crowd protection whatever! Thanks largely to the skill of drivers of the faster cars, the day ended without incident and was a huge success — and driving the '2.3' to and from the event was something still to be remembered.

By now, sales at the garage were taking an upward swing and among new customers was a Mr. John Gaul who bought for re-sale three cars, the SS100 Jaguar two-seater, the '2.6' MG saloon and, rather surprisingly, Hugh Hunter's single seater Alta while, at almost the same time Guy Salmon bought the Monza type '2.3' Alfa, making rather a deep hole in the stock and me without a 'racer'. I wondered whether Robin Jackson still had the Alta I'd driven for him before the war and, finding that he had, I solved that problem by paying him a visit and buying it. Interest was being shown, parti-

cularly from overseas, in both Rolls Royce and Bentleys and the first stock replacement was an early Van Vooren saloon bodied 4.1/4 litre Bentley first registered in 1934 though the 4.1/4 didn't, in fact, go into production until eighteen months later. Frank Kennington, from whom I bought it, told me that it was, in fact, a prototype with the larger and later engine in a 3½ litre chassis. I searched for a good but not over-priced Rolls, in the end finding a very pretty Freestone & Webb sports saloon-bodied 1932, 20/25hp, which I used for some time before deciding that I liked it so much that, when it sold, I would get another, similar but two years later and with steering wheel Ride control. By the time the 1932 car sold, I had found the one I wanted, a 1934 20/25 Sports Saloon, H.J. Mulliner-bodied, registered AYR199, a really lovely and rather pretty car which I kept for a long time. This, with the Low Chassis 4½ litre Invicta, KLL437 and a 1939 Fiat 500 Cabriolet, constituted our family fleet for years.

Life by now had become very busy, for the Bugatti Owner's Club had succeeded in getting Prescott operating again and finding

The first post war event organised by 'Rivers' Rivers-Fletcher. Officially described as a 'Parade of Racing and Sports Cars' it quickly became rather more competitive. The event was on a building site at Cockfosters. Crowd control was 'informal'. Charles and Jean Mortimer brought this fine 2.3 litre Alfa Romeo.

that George Abecassis and John Heath were competing with Altas, we put in a late entry and went as well, towing the single seater on a self-steering bar behind the Invicta and staying at the Lillie Brook Hotel in Cheltenham. Driving the Alta from Cheltenham to Prescott, on trade plates but sans wings and with open exhaust in pouring rain next morning sitting in a raging torrent of water from the unguarded twin rear wheel was no fun — and nor was the meeting, for Prescott in the 1940's wasn't as it is today. The rain became even heavier as the day wore on and the mud in the paddock became so deep and glutinous that all hope of getting any power to the road vanished despite lowered tyre pressures and a helpful B.O.C. Member with a hose on the start line. Though our time of 56.70 seconds just beat John's 56.90 with the 2 Litre car, one couldn't beat George's 55.65 with the independently sprung single-seater.

An invitation to lunch a few days later from Geoffrey Taylor, Alta's designer and Managing Director, brought forth the suggestion that we might like to become Alta concessionaires since he, himself wanted to hive off the sales side so as to have more time for design, development and manufacture. Though we had no doubt that, as Alta's number one pre-war driver, George and his firm H.W. Motors had already been offered and turned it down, we accepted, provided we didn't actually have to stock even one Alta as demonstrator. This hiccup was resolved on the basis of our ordering one of the first of the post-war single-seater Grand Prix models. It was also agreed that until the new car became available, we would continue to run at as many meetings as possible with our pre-war car and that, in return, he would give us all the help and support we needed — excepting money! We tried hard to implement our side of the agreement, winning our class at the Speed Trials held on the seafront at Hartlepool, including

It was only rarely that Geoffrey Taylor (who wanted Charles Mortimer to become the agent for his Alta competition cars) ever competed in his own cars. Here he is at Shelsey Walsh in 1947.

Jean Mortimer in 1946 driving the Alta for the first time won the Ladies Class at Shelsey Walsh.

higher capacity classes and making Fastest Time of Day. Though Jean had never previously driven the car apart from a short run on the road early one morning from Cobham to Ripley and back, she put up Fastest Ladies time and won the Ladies Challenge Trophy at the June 1946 Shelsley Walsh Hill Climb with 50.69 secs to my 47.2secs again in pouring rain. This lasted all day, turning the red Worcestershire soil into a mudbath which, in turn, changed the colour of the car from being green.

After a few more Hill Climb meets like this, we decided to wait until the circuit racing resumed since there was already talk about negotiations being held to stage one at Gransden Lodge near Cambridge and rumblings about possible new circuits in Sussex and Northamptonshire. This brought about another meeting with Geoffrey, first

to request information about progress of the new Grand Prix car and when that seemed to have come to a halt due to difficulties of supply, to ask to be released from continuing to use the pre-war car in races and to get something a bit less temperamental for circuit racing which now seemed almost round the corner. He was good about this and agreed at once with the proviso that when the new car was ready, we would use that only, to which we agreed.

We took our first Continental holiday with the Rolls to see the Swiss Grand Prix at Geneva, the first post-war Grand Prix to be held. In retrospect, I don't recall quite how we did it, for we stayed at the Hotel des Bergues alongside the lake and at the time, by Government decree, the maximum allowance for foreign travel amounted to £50 per person. There had been one or two

SHELSLEY WALSH
5th. October. 1946

small races previously, mainly in France, in which a few British drivers had competed and we certainly did get some useful tips from them, mainly that money shortage could largely be offset by barter with things that the French desperately needed. Though we did make a list at the time, it's hard to recall everything but we certainly loaded the Rolls with many tyre inner tubes and with shoes, both of many different sizes, and with chocolate and confectionery for the children and returned with all of it gone.

Though the 20/25hp Rolls was marvellously comfortable, it was anything but fast and since we weren't in a hurry anyway, we just jogged along in gorgeous weather, stopping whenever we spotted an attractive looking bistro. One's first reaction was horror at the sight of Boulogne harbour and the devastation at that part of the town.

Though originally we'd planned to use the services of either the A.A. or R.A.C. for the documentation aspect — and at that time there was rather a lot of it! — we'd been recommended the travel firm of Autocheques whose Mr. Bird turned out to be a pillar of strength. He recommended us to stop the first night at the Chateau de Montreuil where we dined and slept in luxury long since unseen in Britain and next morning we set off for Paris where we stopped again for the night, for the scenes en route were so staggering that we felt we must see it all. Towns and villages seemed to be making a remarkable recovery but out in the country the desolation was appalling, with wrecked tanks, gun carriers and lorries by the roadside everywhere. Many bridges were down both in the towns and outside and at one point not only a wrecked railway bridge but also a giant railway locomotive blocked the road, necessitating a twenty mile detour through winding unsignposted roads. But, everywhere, French hospitality and cuisine seemed just as before.

The first great highlight of the trip was, one evening, to spot the lights of Geneva on the way down from the Jura mountains while Britain was still only recovering slowly from the effects of the wartime blackout; the second was the shops themselves, stocked to bursting point with everything that had long since vanished from our shops at home. The result of this was that two hours of window shopping had to be done before checking in at the 'Des Bergues'. At the time, it seemed no words could describe adequately Geneva itself and, particularly, the hotel, the whole thing amounting to a quick 'flashback' to the standards that one could barely afford in 1939. To conserve finance, we only slept and breakfasted in the hotel, buying our wine, cheese and pâté from the numerous delicatessens and having picnics in the Jura foothills where, on the first day and by pure luck we came across a tiny, remote little restaurant situated actually in a farmyard, displaying a menu so exciting that we returned to try it that evening. Though the combination of farmyard and restaurant seems rather bizarre it was all so cleverly planned that neither encroached on the other. Dinner that evening, and its almost absurdly modest price, made us regular customers for the rest of our stay.

Four Type 159 Alfa Romeos driven by Farina, Wimille, Varzi and Count Trossi and two 4.CL Maseratis driven by Nuvolari and Villoresi formed the hardcore of the race supported by lesser Continental drivers and a small contingent of British, including Reg Parnell, made up the field. The circuit ran through the suburbs of the town. We watched every practice being able, thanks to Reg, to get into the pits; this even seemed possible without passes although we were glad of them on race day. Officialdom was at its minimum and, by the end of practice it became obvious that despite the presence of the 'Maestro' the Maseratis, which weren't even the post-war 4 CLTs were going to have their work cut out to score over the Alfas.

There was drama almost right from the start. This took place on quite a wide section of road before a right turn into a rather narrow one with high stone walls and a pavement on which was mounted at least one lamp post. No sooner had the leaders poured in a bright red flood into the side road that panic seemed to break out among the marshals and officials at the junction, panic so great that one had the strong feeling that someone might have forgotten about the lamp post or been crowded inextricably onto the pavement. And one wouldn't have been wrong because when, next round, led by Wimille, there were only three Alfas split by one Maserati one had a pretty good idea of what had happened; and from the torrent of beautiful invective that flowed between the Alfa and Maserati pits, one gathered that Nuvolari was getting the blame. While Villoresi was no longer on the scene, it was the 'litle man' who was splitting the Alfas throughout the race, his obviously slower car sounding rough at half distance, rougher still a bit later before black oil began to leak from the bonnet louvres, apparently spelling the end. Lapped at the one hairpin by Wimille, the nose of the Maserati apparently touched the tail of the Alfa, spinning it through a hundred and eighty degrees and this started another shouting match in the pits as Wimille came past quite a long way behind the other two Alfas, side by side with Nuvolari, the Maser with its dented radiator grille and the Alfa with its scored tail.

Ten laps or so later Wimille, now leading his team crossed the line a winner with Nuvolari quite a long way back now, his car more black then red and seeming to be on one cylinder only. A lap later, they all came in, Tazio stopping dead at his pit, leaping out and vaulting the pit counter, curling up beneath it like a little monkey and swilling mineral water from a bottle handed to him by his mechanic. Tremendous drama followed starting with boos from the crowd in the grandstand opposite the pit, some of whom, led by a man brandishing an umbrella, got on to the road. Tazio's mechanic met them half way armed with a jack handle, just as Alfa personnel arrived at the Maserati pit finding it apparently empty since, being at the front of the pit, the culprit couldn't be seen beneath the counter. As the man with the umbrella dealt his first swipe, Tazio's one supporter deftly grabbed the umbrella, flinging it down the road and grabbing his jack handle. This, and the arrival of officials and police quelled the disturbance apart from very small and sporadic outbursts, all non-violent but argumentative. Comedy at its best, in fact. Just great!

Next day, though we would have liked to have stayed longer, we headed the Rolls for home, the only incident being one unscheduled stop on coming across an apparently broken down racing car transporter which turned out to be only overheated. The car had retired early in the race with a broken conrod which had come out through the side of the crankcase. Though the damage looked appalling, the owner, whose name I don't recall, didn't seem too downcast. "Yes, it doesn't look very nice, does it. But I do have a spare case — and I shall show a profit on the trip anyway because I've removed the rotors of the supercharger and stuffed the casing with Swiss watches — and the induction pipe as well. All the area is sealed with 'Locktite' and Customs will be so horrified at the sight of the crankcase that they just won't bother to look any further." We thanked him and left, feeling that we really couldn't add to his troubles even if

we'd thought of doing so.

It turned out to be just as well that we hadn't stayed on in Geneva because within an hour of being back in the office next day, a 'phone call came from America confirming not only that, in response to our semi-display advertisement of the 1932 Rolls '20/25' in *Motor Sport,* the car was sold but that there was a strong demand for good, attractively-bodied pre-war Rolls Royces there and that the buyer would want several more if this one came up to expectations, which we felt sure it would. And there had been a call from George Abecassis asking for an urgent call back. The gist of George's news was that it was now almost certain that a race was going to be held at Gransden Lodge airfield circuit and that it would almost certainly be in July, the one proviso being that the circuit would first have to be approved by and R.A.C. Steward, in this case Earl Howe. He, George, had been asked to meet the Earl up there in three days time, armed with a fairly fast car in which they both could, together, lap the circuit fairly briskly. He was going to do it with the two litre supercharged Sports two-seater Alta — and would I like to go with him? I said "Yes" adding that, at the garage, we had a pre-war T.T. Replica chain-drive Frazer Nash on which we had just completed work. The owner, who was at Cambridge University, had first given me news that there might be a meeting there and, if so, would be on the organising Committee so, if George didn't mind, we could meet at Gransden, deliver the car and return together in the Alta. "Fine Charlie, but let's go up in convoy. Wouldn't a 'chaingang' Frazer Nash hamper the Alta a bit? Well you can only do your best, old boy. But we'll make an early start anyway."

The run to Gransden went well and, never having driven one for any distance before, it was a new experience. Slightly lacking maximum but great on corners once one got used to it, the Nash did have the Alta sitting on its tail most of the way, especially on the long straights nearer the circuit. The owner was pleased with what had been done and there was a great welcome from 'The Noble Lord', standing waiting and chatting to officials beside his '57 SC' Bugatti coupe, DYK5. "Well done George, you've made good time. Now let's have a look at this circuit." As he climbed into the passenger seat, the Earl pulled out his goggles and George, his cap back to front, muttered to me "Now we'll frighten the Old Man, Charlie." But not all old men are easily frightened and as they came in after five surprisingly fast laps, the Earl was laughing heartily. "Great, George. Nothing wrong with that. We'll do it." Though it's difficult to remember after forty years every detail of a fast run, two things apart from the speed, stand out, the first being the 2 Litre's exhaust note particularly when accelerating hard and the second, our passage through one fairly large town where, unseen by George, a police car was emerging from a side street, its occupants leaning forward with interest. It turned to follow us as I warned him. "O.K. old boy, give the Ki-Gas three hard shoves." I did and, looking

A study of Charles Mortimer in the 4 CM Maserati before the start of the first post war circuit race at Gransden Lodge in Norfolk.

behind, saw just a thick black fog of exhaust smoke which, when it cleared, revealed a diminishing dot in the distance.

The search for a suitable mount for the Gransden Meeting ended with the purchase of the lovely little 1½ Litre single-seater Maserati Type 4.C that had been driven so successfully by the late Teddy Rayson, not quite as fast as a good ERA but with a wonderful record for reliability. The car itself is illustrated opposite page 104 in Anthony Pritchard's book, *Maserati — a History* with, below, an independently sprung Type 6.C that I subsequently bought to replace it after selling the 4.C to Roy Salvadori. The comic thing about this was that the caption below the 6.C reads: "Le Mans winner, Tony Rolt with the 6.CM which he drove in British events soon after the end of the second world war."

The photograph of the 'six' is reproduced on the dust wrapper and when I wrote to the publishers pointing out not only that the driver was me and not Tony, who never at any time drove a Maserati, I got no reply — and none to any other letter I subsequently wrote, either from the publishers or from the author. But when, in the end, I sent them a copy of the photograph, reproduced from the negative, which was my property and hadn't even been acknowledged, I got a reply immediately! A much more satisfactory one than I expected! I replied by return, thanking them and saying that had they acknowledged the mistake earlier, I would have been more than happy just to have been featured on the dust wrapper below the print of Stirling Moss!

No sooner had I bought the 4.C than I was offered a 3 litre single-seater eight cylinder, the '8C' by Reg Parnell who, while others were buying pre-war racing cars. Reg and I had kept in touch throughout the war, mainly due to the fact that he had continued to run, with his brother Bill, their family business, Standard Transport up in Derby and since his big vehicles ran fairly regularly down to London, we at Fairmile were often glad to give them return loads back to the Midlands and the North. The car he was now offering me was one that had been raced on the Continent by Count Villapadierna and after some time spent in price negotiation, I bought that as a stable mate to the 4.C.

The greatest problem at that time was the one of driving or testing a racing car for, Gransden apart, there were no circuits open which meant that one had to seek a friendly disused aerodrome. But we tested the '8C' another way, taking it early one summer morning by van to a nearby stretch of mainly uninhabited main road about ten miles long where, on trade plates, we ran it slowly outwards and fairly fast back; then, by the roadside, we set about changing plugs for a faster run. This was about five o'clock in the morning and as we worked on the car we noticed a large house shrouded by trees. Suddenly we were confronted by an elderly gent clad in dressing gown and pyjamas and clearly angry. He roared up menacingly: "What in Heaven's name is going on. A racing car — and at this time of the morning? D'you know what you've done? I run a boy's school here — and you've woken me and two hundred of my pupils." Starting to reload the car in the transporter prior to a quick exit, we apologised. "No. Don't take it away. You've woken us all now, so do another run and meanwhile I'll bring the little blighters out to watch. At their age, they've never seen a racing car." So, to a large and admiring dressing-gowned audience we did two more runs — one more than we needed.

It was a very nice car indeed, so nice that a short test decided us to keep it and re-sell its smaller brother. But the fates were against it. Later that day, Reg 'phoned again, this time to say that he had a customer with him who had come specially to see the car and who said he 'had to have it' which I took

A historic moment in motor racing history. The start of the first official post war motor race at Gransden. The Maserati is 2nd from the right.

to mean that Reg might possibly have fallen into the dealers trap of offering the same car to two different people without naming a price to either, something that can happen if the first choice is slow to respond. I really did want to keep it and offered instead the '4C' which was promptly rejected. I said to Reg "Are you over a barrel on this one?" and he replied "Yes." Taking a deep breath, I named a price, to cover Reg and compensate myself — a price that I felt must be unacceptable. But it wasn't and early next morning one of Standard Transport's smallest and fastest vehicles was on the doorstep, its driver armed with a cheque. My disappoint-

ment lasted for just one week when I tried the 4.C for the first time at a small airfield near Odiham. In another book, I later described the 4.C as "the nicest racing car I ever owned" — and it was. Not as fast as its big brother who I'd never really grown to know, it was light, responsive, forgiving and above all 'friendly' with no feeling of fierceness and, enormously willing. The test, though longer than that of the 3 Litre, wasn't really long but just enough to get to know it until practice on the day.

We went up to Gransden the day before the race and walked the course as dusk fell. No problems in practice, good weather and a big crowd The event, the main one of the day for the Gransden Trophy was a 22 lapper and the distance 44 miles. The field was good, too, with Poore's big 3.8 Litre Alfa Grand prix car, Hutchinson's and Salvadori's '2.9' Monopostos, Harrison's and Heath's ERAs, George Abecassis' Type 59 3.3 Litre G.P. Bugatti, Kenneth Bear's 3 Litre, Yates '2.3', McAlpine's 3 Litre Maserati, Leslie Johnson's big 4 Litre Darracq and various others — eighteen starters in all.

Unfortunately the start was at the beginning of the long straight which gave the big cars rather an advantage over the others on sheer power alone. But, amazingly, at the end of the first lap only Poore, Abecassis, Salvadori and Rolt's and Hutchinson's Alfas lay ahead, all of them still in view — and all three litre or over. It was a situation that seemed too good to be true though, looking in the mirror, the others led by McAlpine and the two ERAs seemed to be dropping back. We latched onto the tail of Hutchinson's Monoposto, comfortably outbraking it into the hairpin on several occasions though it's extra litreage made it pull away after the exit

until on lap six, it retired in a cloud of smoke leaving us to fight for — and lose — fourth place to Leslie's big Darracq at the finish, but with all the others except Poore still in sight. The fact that this was the first race meeting in Britain for nearly seven years must have been the reason for Bill Boddy's eulogistic report of the race in *Motor Sport* — ''This was quite the finest race we have seen or shall see in England this year. Poore, the winner led throughout, Abecassis' '3.3' Bugatti was second, Salvadori third, Johnson fourth with Mortimer holding onto the Darracq's tail, fifth. We timed Poore to lap at nearly 88mph on his seventh lap, Salvadori at 84.51 and Mortimer at 81.00 in the 1½ litre ex-Rayson Maserati. This strikes us as a memorable drive, particularly as this old 8-valve car easily disposed of the ERAs.''

I think that Roy Salvadori must have made rather a good sale of the Alfa as a result of this race because, from records I still have, it was then that he bought the 4.C from me — also at a good price! At the time, he and I were doing quite a lot of mutual business, most of it, I think, to his advantage rather

The Alta (on the inside) has just been missed by Peter Whitehead's wildly spinning ERA as has the famous ERA Delage, driven on this occasion by Tim Parnell.

than mine so the fact that he had made a good sale of the Monoposto must have been the reason for his generosity to me! But right from his early days, trading in Warren Street, Roy was always a marvellous man with whom to deal — shrewd but as straight as a die and, from time to time, generous, as this little episode shows! I liked everything about the old Maserati except two things, its preselector gearbox and its age which made me feel that having been so good and reliable for so long, the day couldn't be far distant when its crankshaft would break and I didn't want this to happen while I owned it. At the time, Charlie Brackenbury was offering me a good Maserati Type 6.C, a much later car with 1½ Litre six cylinder engine and with independent front suspension so, though it had been raced in Britain and its history wasn't known, I tried it and bought it.

It was with this car that I had one of the wierdest events of my life as a dealer. Looking after the car was Les Wilson, one of the 'great' pre-war mechanics who had been for years with Thompson and Taylor at Brooklands and who, that day, was being aided by Gerry Belton who then worked for me at Byfleet. The meeting was being held at Stanmer Park near Brighton and up the long private drive to the house. The first quarter mile was straight, tree-lined and with wide grass verges and this served as the paddock while the second quarter was twisty and rather bumpy to the finish. The car went well and put up quite a good time in practice and we were just about to go the the beer tent for a drink when a man and a woman hove in sight and said that they would like to buy it — and what was the price? We named it and they each wrote out a cheque for half a share. But then came the snag because it turned out that having got that far, he was expecting to take over and to drive it at the meeting. He saw the point and immediately named a competitor who was a well-known motor trader who, so he said, would stand behind both cheques but sadly our mutual friend would only stand

The 6 CM Maserati which replaced the 4CM. Pictured here at Stanmer Park Speed Trials in 1947.

behind the man's cheque and not the lady's as well. So that was that, but they urged me to drive it on their behalf which in the end I did, with some reserve because having sold it, I wanted to keep it in one piece. I then went to have a drink, telling Les and Gerry that if either 'buyer' wanted to sit in the car, they could but on no account to let them start it. So I was a bit shocked when, ten minutes later, the car came roaring down the drive scattering people in all directions, the 'buyer' at the wheel with Les and Gerry on foot some hundreds of yards astern, doing the fastest quarter mile they'd done in their lives. I joined in and we came across the Maserati embedded in a nettle-infested earth bank with the 'buyer' sat at the wheel and considerably shaken. Luckily, no serious damage had been done apart from the fact that we put the cheques into the bank the next day, both were returned marked 'R/D'!

One of our customers at this time, also a Maserati owner, was Alastair Baring with whom I had talks about a business merger; this ended in an exchange of shares in our garage business for an equal number in his home-grown timber and builders' merchant's businesses though this didn't last very long for various reasons. At this time I was becoming rather disenchanted with motor racing, mainly because of the dearth of circuit racing but also because of the escalated cost of competing with a racing car which involved transport and personnel, all of which made me start to think about racing a good sports car. Healys had produced and raced the new two-seater 'Silverstone' model so when, one day, Baring told me that he'd bought from them the car that Tony Rolt had driven in the 1949 Production Sports Car Race at Silverstone and could I possibly go up to the works at Warwick and collect it, I did so, liking it more the further I drove it.

Stopping for a coffee and a sandwich, I made some notes on the car which I thought would interest its new owner, who was standing on the front steps of the office as I drove in. This particular meeting was to tell me a lot about him that, at that time, I didn't know, for without further ado his opening words were "Do you think you could sell that for me. I don't want it." I knew, by then, that I was going to buy a 'Silverstone' anyway and asked him to name a price, which he did. "No. I do know someone who wants a Silverstone but not at that price or even near it." He named another price and I wrote out a cheque and gave it to him. I asked him why he was selling it and he'd found a faster, better car, a Le Mans replica Frazer Nash which certainly was faster and better but, at the time, far far more expensive.

From that time on I realised that where cars were concerned, he was erratic and indecisive, one of those people who thought that success in motor racing was just a matter of getting the fastest possible car without even considering their ability to get the best out of it by improving their driving with experience. I collected the Frazer Nash next day, thought it one of the loveliest cars of its type I'd ever driven and he drove it in an event the following weekend with no success, asking me to return it, two days later, to Roy Salvadori, whence it had come, with a message to say that it lacked acceleration and maximum speed. Roy took it back without question, ran it two weekends later at Shelsley, and broke the two litre Sports Car record for the Hill with it. He supplied in its place my old 4.C 1½ Litre Maserati single-seater which, in its turn, produced no results of note for the Baring stable, and was traded later for a 2½ Litre HWM prior to a season's racing in Grand Prix events on the Continent ending with the Jersey International Road Race. The HWM, a new car, didn't figure in any results one could find in the 'dailies' or even in the motoring press but after a time, it's owner arrived back in

Typical of early post war racing. The 2½ litre Riley engined Healey at Blandford Camp. The car was also used for shopping.

a trememdous hustle. "Charles, old boy, business has escalated so much while I've been away that I can't possibly stay away any longer. Buckle has gone ahead with the car to Jersey. How would you feel about driving the car in the race?" I felt that I'd like to very much. I knew and liked Buckle the mechanic, an enormously patient and easy going young man who, when at base, worked immaculately attired on the cars one day and up to his ankles in mud on the tractors that pulled the timber drags the next. I wanted a break from it all and this seemed the opportunity so I took, with Jean, the night boat to Jersey.

On arrival, I sought out Buckle whose opening words were: "Hello, how are you? Glad to hear you're going to drive. HWMs have been very good and I think we're over the trouble now." "What trouble? I didn't know you'd had any." he looked rather embarassed. "Well, no, we haven't ourselves actually. But the works cars which are identical seem to have run into a little patch of shedding wheels. Stirling was one. I'm not sure who the others were. But our car now

has the same mods as theirs."

Not even having seen the car till then and due to practise with it that afternoon, I sat in it and explored. It was the last of the first batch, the body wider than the later ones, and with its 2½ litre unblown engine, a very nice little car. The afternoon practice confirmed first impressions and nothing shook loose — not even the wheels. Whereas I'd been led to believe that, with no blower, we could go through the race non-stop, Buckle was rather doubtful so we gathered up the equipment and rehearsed a pit stop together. The course was great — a long blind down the wide seafront with, at the end, a sharp right hander into a rather narrow shop-lined section, curving to the right, straightening and widening for the run back through the town with an occasional twisty bit just to make it interesting and ending in a slow righthand hairpin back on to the front. With so little practice our times hadn't been spectacular, maybe because I was spending too much time focusing on the wheels and stub axles! Pure lack of dedication — a top driver would have shrugged it off and thought no more about it whereas to me the shop windows looked hard and uninviting.

The field, though not enormous, was very high quality with the new '4CLT' Maseratis being driven by Reg, David Hampshire, Baron de Graffenreid and 'Bira', ERAs by Graham Whitehead, Brian Shaw-Taylor, Cuth Harrison and Bob Gerard, earlier Maseratis by David Murray, Joe Ashmore and Duncan Hamilton with a 6C, sharing the driving with Philip Fotheringham Parker and other 'makeweights' with Tony Rolt's ex-Seaman Delage, two of the new Alta G.P. cars with Joe Kelly and Geoffrey Crossley, two Vee-Twin JAP-engined Coopers, neither of which lasted long, Branca's Simca and the HMWs.

On the grid, we were directly behind Duncan's 'Maser', alongside one of the Altas; our best practice time had been 83mph exactly to the Ferrari's 93.5. At the fall of the flag the 'Maser's' rear wheels disappeared in a black cloud of rubberdust and the car slid sideways, dealing Merrick's Cooper quite a cruel blow. But it all cleared quite quickly as the field strung out along the seafront, becoming rather a traffic jam again at the right hander as everyone funnelled into the narrow part. Initially we

Something of a 'quiz' photograph. Earl Howe introducing the Governor to the drivers at the Jersey International Road Races. The author (third from right) talking to the Governor. Others present include; Tony Rolt, Bob Gerard, Philip Fotheringham-Parker, Ray Merrick, Farina, De Graffenreid, Duncan Hamilton (head only). The author believes that Peter Whitehead is in there somewhere as he won!

sat on the Maserati's tail with no difficulty because, despite Duncan's lurid driving, the car didn't seem fast. Though everyone was using pavements now and then, he seemed to be more on them than the road itself through the town and it only took a couple of laps to make one feel sure that this couldn't last. So, dropping back so as not to be involved when whatever was going to happen did happen, I watched it all with admiration. Going through the narrow bit on the third lap, the car swiped the offside kerb and, with its rear wheels spinning madly, bounced back across the road, just missing the Post Office, spun through a hundred and eighty degrees and continued quite fast backwards with Duncan, puce in the face, fighting it all the way.

Years later Duncan said in his great book *Touch Wood* that "Charles Mortimer passed me going rather more slowly forwards than I was going backwards" and that was true because till then there'd been no room to pass him at all! After that, a clear road all the way, an almost race long personal duel with Branca's quick little Simca and a lot of time spent looking into the mirror so as not to hold up faster cars through the town. By the standards of the day the fuel stop was reasonable, taking 25 seconds to put in ten gallons from a churn, and it was only on the very last lap that the car became suddenly sick and limped to the finish to finish tenth, one second ahead of the Simca. Peter Whitehead's Ferrari won in 1 hour 56 mins 2.6 secs with the Maseratis of Reg and De Graf-

Charles Mortimer leading Joe Kelly's Alta driving Alastair Baring's HWM during the race.

fenreid second and third, the winning speed being 90.94mph. Even with not a very fast car, it was great to be driving in such wonderful company. Baffled by the last lap misfiring, the wonderful Buckle quickly diagnosed a punctured carburettor float and the car then drove back to its garage in the hotel in a ladylike manner.

Back to Normal

Back at home, we had a big switch round of cars. The V-12 Lagonda was a lovely car, faster and quieter than a 4.1/4 litre Bentley but enormously thirsty fuelwise at a time when petrol was still scarce. And it had one irritating quirk which no one seemed able to cure — it could be a pig to start when hot, especially in hot weather. It chose to do this on my wedding day when, with Jean's brother, Patrick we had stopped for just one quick one at the White Lion at Cobham on the way to 'tying the knot.' In the end, it did start but one felt all the time that it well might not after the service! So that was it's swansong!

George Abecassis lent me a Citroen 'Light Fifteen', ostensibly for a day though it only took a forty mile run to fall in love with it. It was a super little car but coloured black, so, having noticed that many of the Paris taxis were black Citroens with yellow wheels, we brightened its rather sombre appearance by painting its wheels yellow as well. This car was the first of several Citroens, being followed by one of the fairly scarce 2 litres 'Sixes' and later still by a super, little 'Light Fifteen' two-seater Drophead Coupe. None of them gave any trouble and all covered big mileages.

My daily 'home to office' journey at this time was from Weybridge, via Byfleet to Bracknell and every morning I used to meet Duncan Hamilton doing the same journey in reverse. I was seeing quite a lot of Duncan at the time, mostly at race meetings where we were both competing. Though not as

well known as he later became, he was fast but rather 'hairy' and tended to have prangs, so that some time previously he had formed a mythical 'Club' which one could only join having had a prang oneself. Whenever I saw him he was always urging me to qualify for membership usually with the words "Go on Charles, time you joined the Club. Have a really good one. You'll drive much better after it."

One morning, rather late for the office, I was pressing on in the Citroen 'Six' and did have a big one, collecting broadside a Ferguson tractor with trailer which turned right into a gateway without warning, wrecking the car so completely that the nearside front wheel was pushed so far back that it almost prevented the door from opening. And while I was giving my version of the accident to the police, who should roll up but Duncan? Surveying the scene with a broad grin he said in a loud voice "Well done Charles old boy, well done. Jeepers what a mess. And look at those bloody skid marks. What speed were you doing? Life Membership old boy." And that, more than anything else, got me a dangerous driving charge, changed to 'without due care' on my agreeing to plead guilty. It was some time before I forgave him for that because, till he'd arrived and commented, the police had almost been on my side, and seemed not to have noticed the skid marks.

By this time both Goodwood and Silverstone circuits were entities even though with almost no facilities initially, for both had

What happened to the author's 2 litre Citroen Six when it met a Ferguson tractor. Duncan Hamilton's arrival on the scene definitely did not help.

been wartime airfields. Though both were welcomed gratefully by enthusiasts like ourselves, it was Goodwood, the property of the Duke of Richmond, that somehow seemed to have inherited the mantle of Brooklands, partly because the Duke himself had been a successful Brooklands driver, partly because the Committee was made up of old B.A.R.C. Members but also because, like Brooklands it somehow seeemed to have pre-war atmosphere. Starting initially with Club meetings, it soon sprouted pits and administrative buildings and, going on to stage International events, really did seem to have become the post-war Brooklands. Fairly early on, George Abecassis and I were invited to serve on the Events Committee, and, later, were promoted to the Council itself. Both, and particularly the Council, were made up of eminent pre-war person-alities, some of whom had raced successfully while nearly all had motor trade backgrounds.

Inevitably, all were elderly and, though quite progressive, seemed to adhere to the Brook-lands tradition of 'The Right Crowd and No Crowding.' George and I, hailed as 'the younger members', tended not to speak unless spoken to and I well recall two occasions particularly when we did.

The first when the programme for one of the early Goodwood Bank Holiday meetings was being thrashed out on a rather limited financial budget, the problems being what sort of a programme would hold best appeal and how best to divide the fairly small sum of available start money among competitors. Various not very inspiring ideas were put forward and rejected until one eminent member came forward with the suggestion that the programme should consist of just one nine hour race for saloon cars exactly as supplied to the public and with limits on fuel consumption based on the makers' claims. George wrote on his pad two words only: 'Piss Poor.' He handed the pad to me and I agreed that nothing could be duller. Seeing this, the Chairman said: "Ah, now, I see the younger members have some thoughts on this. Charles, you have an idea perhaps?" I said I hadn't but agreed with the note that my friend George felt about the Nine Hour idea — which put George fairly and squarely in the hot seat. Pressed to say just what he thought, George said "Well, I don't know how best to put it but, frankly, I can't think of anything less exciting than a nine hour touring car race. If you want my opinion, for what it's worth, I'd put on a programme of short handicaps for various classes and types with a twenty or twenty five lap Scratch Race for racing cars unlimited and give all the start money to one top-notch Italian driver, whose name should end with an 'a' or 'i', driving the latest blood-red Italian single-seater available, preferably a driver who's just taken off with some other driver's wife so that all our potential spectator's wives will want to come as well, just to see what she looks like." And they did it, booking Nino Farina who brought over a 4.CLT Maserati, fitted the definition in every way except the last, won the race and drew the biggest gate Goodwood had ever seen till then.

My first real contribution came later. At that time, one could only get a new car by signing a covenant agreeing not to sell it for, I think, two years from the date of purchase, the idea being that since new cars were even then hard to get, this would prevent profit taking. A certain post-war driver, a motor trader, looked into this covenant thing with his lawyer to find that the covenant wasn't in any way a legally binding document. Thereby, he made a lot of money. Very much an up-and-coming driver, he had applied to join the Club in order to race at Goodwood — and had his application turned down. He had asked me if there was anything I could do to get the decision

reversed. I'd done many deals with him on pre-war cars and found him great to deal with. He'd not broken any laws but had only found a loophole and I felt sure that if he remained barred, the day could come when the Club would want him at Goodwood, perhaps invite him and find their invitation refused. So I told John Morgan I'd like to get the Council's decision reversed at the next meeting. John was horrified. "Charles, that's a real hot potato. I'm sure they won't consider it. But I'll tell you how we can try. Council meetings end at eight o'clock and they like to be in the bar by eight fifteen. We'll bring it up right at the end of the meeting under the heading 'Any other Business.' That'll prevent it being mulled over for hours."

He was as good as his word. To a rather shocked silence, the Chairman, the charming and almost paternal Professor Low, asked me on what grounds I made the request and I said that as a car dealer of thirty years standing I'd dealt on numerous occasions with the applicant, found him always helpful, honest and trustworthy, emphasising that apart from finding a loophole in the law, he hadn't broken it and ended by saying that, as a driver myself, I'd competed against him and was convinced that though, at that time, he was only starting to climb the ladder, I was as sure as I possibly could be that before long he would become a very good driver indeed and possibly a great one who would be in demand everywhere and if barred at Goodwood now might one day refuse an invitation to drive there if it came. There was a brief discussion and rather to my surprise there was a reversal of the decision by a big majority — and the applicant not only became a big name internationally but was welcomed at Goodwood and won numerous big events there.

The Healey 'Silverstone' gave us enormous fun throughout 1950, winning numerous Club events and notching up places almost

Jean Mortimer at the wheel of their first Healey has a few cheerful words with Charles before the start of a race at Goodwood in 1950.

everywhere we went with it, besides being an acceptable shopping car and great for a quick run down to the coast. For most of that season, our 'Silverstone' OPA 2 seemed fairly well able to hold off the opposition of other Silverstones but all that ended in August when in the B.R.D.C. Production Sports Car Race 'curtain raiser' to the British Grand Prix, the works produced a 1950 model to be driven by Duncan Hamilton. Practice on the first day saw the XK120 Jaguars of Tony Rolt and Peter Walker fastest at 81.24mph with Duncan's and our Healeys next with 79.38mph. Quite encouraging but it didn't last for, next day, Cuth Harrison with Warburton's big Cadillac-engined Allard came top with 85.24, Duncan 4th at 80.69 and ours fifth with 79.99.

Had it not been for Duncan our speed wouldn't have bettered our previous effort because we had practised and put the car away when Duncan came along shouting "Quick, get in your car, we're going out again. Nuvolari's practising with the XK120 — not much faster than our cars. Follow me and with a bit of luck you may be able to tell your grandchildren one day that you passed the great Nuvolari — we'll have a shot at it anyway." Though, thanks to Duncan, we did pass the 'Great little Man' we didn't realise, at the time, how ill he was or how soon he was going to die. In the race itself, the Aston Martins of Raymond Somner, Reg Parnell and Eric Thompson were faster than our car but Duncan's skill and determination brought him home ahead of them to win the 3 Litre class at an average of 79.92mph followed by Somner, Reg and Eric second, third, fourth and our car fifth, at 76.61 mph the first privately owned finisher in the class. Though, at the time, it all seemed fairly satisfactory, it was food for thought when, in 1985, I saw Rosberg lap the same circuit — with a chicane added — at 160mph. He was doing two laps in the same time as our one!

Our one big trouble came when, as a precaution, we decided to have the brakes of the Healey re-lined for the T.T. Race in Ireland. Dunlops in London hadn't got the right linings in stock and it was decided to have the job done in Belfast. Foolishly, we practiced quite satisfactorily on the original linings before fitting the new ones for the race. Somehow — we never discovered why — the wrong type linings were fitted and though the car finished seventh in our class, it was brakeless, or nearly, by half distance. Our fault — everything should be tried and tested before the start of a race.

From the time that we arrived for the race in Ireland, it seemed never to stop raining, though never so hard as in the race itself which was run on a time basis of three hours duration. There were one or two little hiccups prior to the race, the first one being heralded by a call on the Tannoy for me to go to the race headquarters tent in the paddock where I was shown the medical certificate my own doctor had filled in before we left home. I hadn't even looked at it before but now it was pointed out to me that in reply to the question 'Does the applicant suffer from giddiness or fits?' he had answered 'Yes.' Promising the doctor present that I certainly didn't, I was asked to close my eyes, stand on one leg and hold the other out horizontally forwards which I didn't do very well because I'd just got out of the car after ten consecutive laps practice in the downpour, was wearing plimsolls and standing on soft muddy grass, so I was advised to see the senior medical officer at the headquarters hotel in Belfast at eight o'clock that evening. When I arrived I was relieved to find him in the bar and rather amused about it and having made his checks, he asked me if I drank? I said "Yes." He punched me in the chest and said "There's nothing wrong with a man who drinks. What's your poison?" and when I said "Scotch" he rocked with laughter and bought me a double.

My dear mother, a born matchmaker and very fond of all Jean's family, had produced the information that, unknown to me, I had an uncle and his son, my cousin, both very horsey people, living not far from Belfast,

adding that we really ought to take Jean's younger sister, Anne, who was also keen on horses because the horse aspect might mean that Anne and my cousin would get on well — so Anne agreed to go with us. So, prior to the race we motored over to meet them and to talk horses. There was great and enjoyable hospitality and everything seemed to be going so well that when it was proposed that Anne should stop the night and go riding next day, she agreed at once. But when we came down to breakfast, there she was, rather to our surprise, the answer to the puzzle being that while my cousin seemed more interested in the horses than in Anne, my uncle had shown more interest in Anne than the horses, hence here rather speedy return by train to Belfast! But, in the end, things did turn out well because, that day, Anne met my Healey team mate, Robin Richards, whom she later married. Today they are still happily married after thirty seven years and living down in Devon — still with horses!

Our tender car for that trip was a Rolls Phantom II Continental saloon, Carlton bodied, coloured gunmetal and very striking with twin rear mounted spare wheels and very elegant flared wings. Driven by Jean it cruised comfortably from Surrey up to Liverpool, in company with the Healey most of the way, at around seventy. The Rolls led the way on the way up but we did it the other way on the return journey in view of the Healey's lack of brakes!

At this stage of the proceedings, big Rolls especially were quite easy to find in good condition and I had such a thriving business in them that there seemed to be less and less time for racing and it was some time after the Healey's departure that we bought our last and smallest racing car, an 1100cc Vee-twin engined single-seater Cooper-JAP, earlier driven by Stirling Moss for the works, rolled by him, rebuilt by the works and put aside where one day we found it. I don't

The author in the ex-Stirling Moss works Cooper JAP 1100 which he bought primarily to learn the Brands Hatch Circuit where he and his equally famous son 'Chas' were running a motor cycle racing school. Here he is competing in a B.R.S.C.C. meeting at the 'Hatch'.

now recall our reason for buying it. I think it must have been that its small size and lightness made it possible to transport it on a trailer behind the car and, perhaps the lingering thought that, after all, racing cars were faster and more exciting to drive than sports. After driving it fairly successfully in the odd Formula Libre race at Brands Hatch and in one or two sprints, it too went on its way. With some regret, the Carlton bodied Phantom II Continental that had taken us to Ireland departed at about the same time. It was always the cars that one liked best that went on their way quickest! Again around this time, I had some talks with Robin Richards following our meeting in Ireland. After leaving the Army, he had joined the ranks of retail motor trade in London's West End, initially in partnership with Dick Carr with whom I'd been at school and with Leonard Potter, who had left the partnership fairly early. But Robin and Dick were running a small but rapidly growing business in good used cars at a

lovely little 'hole-in-the wall' garage in Kinnerton Street, just off Belgrave Square.

At that time they sought someone to join them on a part time basis, with or without a modest investment and, from my point of view it seemed to fit in fairly well with my Rolls Royce activities, since the cars that I was buying almost all went overseas, and the only time I needed was spent in going out in order to buy.

I knew both Robin and Dick well and, since neither had any objection to my continuing to run my 'one man band' with the Rolls thing, I started right away at Kinnerton Street, at first with a small investment and on a 'two days a week' basis. On the whole, it worked rather well to start with. Trading in London was still not fully in its stride following the war and while there were more good, clean cars in the North than in the South, we countered that by stocking the business with cars bought in the North. Any for which there was no room went straight into Southern auctions where they nearly always sold at a respectable profit even taking into account the auctioneer's 'rake off.'

The business had just two fitters whom I only ever knew as 'Dick' and 'Albert'. Both of whom had not only been at school together but had worked together all their lives. They were super chaps and the whole think worked very much as a team. At first we traded mainly in sports cars with the emphasis on Allards, Healeys, Elliott and Abbot bodied, Jaguar XK120s and others with a sporting flavour. Though good relations always existed between management and staff, there were, from time to time, minor 'hiccups' between the partners. One bone of contention was 'Buck', Dick Carr's beautiful bull terrier dog who, if left in any car for more than a few minutes, would chew and demolish, first, the gear lever knob, then the steering wheel and finally any likely looking knobs that protruded from the dash board. Dick always paid for replacements but, as Robin said, it didn't end there because things of that sort could be hard to get and if temporarily unobtainable could immobilise a car and render it unsaleable till replacements arrived.

It didn't end there because with his years of army training behind him, Robin, in his capacity of 'administration', kept voluminous records not only of every deal done but also of almost everything that happened, whereas neither Dick or I were too good at that. I think I was probably a bit better than Dick who, if buying a car, would do a couple of quick laps round Belgrave Square in it, pronounce the deal done, give the owner a cheque, forget to ask for any documents, write the vendor's name and address, but seldom his phone number, on the back of an envelope which he would promptly lose, ultimately driving poor Robin mad while being apologetic but unrepentant! I did try hard to follow the procedures but was only slightly better and neither Dick or I had

much idea of Hire Purchase procedure. We just dealt, leaving procedure to Robin who professed to preferring it.

We did have some strange customers and one of the first arrived when Robin was hard at work in the office at the back end of the showroom and Dick out buying. An elderly, quite prosperous looking chap showed interest in a small Renault and seemed to me to be a possible buyer. After we had chatted together a few minutes, Robin peered through the glass partition, hurriedly scribbled a note and brought it down to me with "Charles, so sorry to disturb you. Could you just cast your eye over that." I did, and it read 'Elderly nutcase — not a hope of selling him anything — has fits and comes in when he feels one coming on. Prelude is to hit his forehead with his right hand. If this happens, get him out pronto."

It did, but it was too late and as Robin knelt, loosening the sufferer's collar, he looked up at me and said "Pity, there just wasn't time was there? But it's not good enough, is it? I've got an idea for a cure." Going out into the road, he stopped the first passer-by with "Excuse me sir, d'you know anything about fits. We've got a gentleman here having one." He went on stopping others till there must have been between twenty and thirty surrounding the patient. Returning to the office he beckoned me. "Right, let's have a cup of tea. That's filled the showroom nicely. Bound to be someone amongst all that lot who'll take over." He was right and we never had another visit from the chap again.

Another, of a different kind, was the 'buyer' of a Kharmann Ghia sports Coupe who tried the car, liked it and gave us a cheque, saying he'd collect it in three days time. Well dressed and with a rather garish old school tie, he was chatty and friendly, regaling us with a lot of information about Kent, where he lived. Rather suspect, so we put the cheque in for special clearance. He was back at nine o'clock, a day ahead of his time, just as Dick and Albert were concluding the car's pre-delivery service. We hadn't had time to get the cheque's clearance so told the boys not to finish the service till the bank opened. But at a quarter to ten he blew up, saying that he could wait no longer but would return next day. But he didn't, because the cheque book he was using was stolen.

Even better was the 'film director' who came specially to see a Vee-12 Lagonda Drophead coupe, bringing with him his 'dolly bird' secretary who thought the car too staid and fell for a bright red XK120 which had proved to be a bit of a 'sticker'. Hopefully, because the Lagonda wasn't an easy car to sell at the time either, Dick suggested having both. "Well now, why didn't we think of that. That's what we'll do. Come round to my flat at six o'clock, all three of you if you'd care to. We'll have drinks ready and tie the thing up." The drinks were only bettered by the flat itself which was opulence personified. But every time Robin produced his Hire Purchase Forms, they were waved away with "Never mind about those. This is the social hour, we'll get down to business later." We all got rather drunk but not as drunk as he did, his 'set piece' being to produce numerous photographs of lovely young ladies to whom he could introduce us and who would give us the most marvellous time we'd ever had! No business ensued but it was agreed that Robin would return with the forms at ten o'clock next morning to tie up the deal. He, the film director, would still be in bed, the hall would be packed with people waiting to see him but Robin was to force a way through and come straight up.

Poor old Robin returned at eleven with his forms completed. "Well, I don't know. There wasn't a soul in the hall but he's completed these so I suppose we'd better put them in." He insisted on putting in two

different lots to two different companies and put the business with the one quoting best. Back to the client who exploded in a big way. Not to worry though, he'd send his Public Relations Officer round within the hour — he'd sort it. The P.R.O. arrived on time, a pimply youth in a black pin-stripe suit and a bowler hat who couldn't sort it because he hadn't been briefed, and in any case, he'd only been working for the 'director' for less than an hour. No reply to the 'phone for the rest of the day — not really surprising because our 'client' had been arrested and charged with embezzlement!

Another series of deals took no end of unravelling. We had a call from the Sales Director of a quite well known firm who were agents for a popular Marque of small car, the gist of it being that since they'd become rather overloaded with 'trade-ins', would we be interested in buying a few, in excellent condition, attractively priced and delivered to our door from the country at no extra charge. We had one, which turned out to be good, then another three and then three more. We had only one left when a roving C.I.D. man called in, whom we knew. He identified the one remaining as being on his list of cars wanted due to hire purchase problems. In his presence we rang the firm to find that not only had it gone bankrupt but that its Sales Director had vanished also. It was a nasty one to sort out — and expensive — not at all the sort of situation in which one would find a Main Agent!

But there weren't so many like these. We had some very nice customers and a very few not quite so nice. One of the latter involved our used car guarantee. More and more small firms like ours were selling used cars under guarantee and we decided we must also. But Robin, always keen to avoid unneccessary expense, decided to bypass the legal bods and draw up a guarantee of his own, his way of doing it being to get copies of a number of guarantees of our competitors and then embody the best points of each in one document. Dick read it and said to me "Read that. No one who read it would ever buy a car from us — except a lunatic." But Robin was adamant and though we did give the guarantee to customers who asked for it, we didn't call on it in cases where the customer was reasonable and his claim justified. One day, however, we came across a customer cast in a different mould. The car he had bought the day before had broken down and would we collect it and rectify the trouble. He hadn't proved to be a nice man to deal with so — over to Robin. "Afraid we can't do that under the terms of our Guarantee. Page two, clause three — the defective part or parts must be removed and brought back to us for our opinion as to whether the Guarantee applies or not. It wouldn't, of course if it were a case of 'fair wear and tear' and, of course, under clause five, our decision on all matters arising from the guarantee is final and binding."

In due course we were sued, the case escalating from one court to another till we stood in front of a Judge in Red Robes, who sagely asked who had drawn up the terms of the Guarantee. Our lawyer named Robin and the judge said "Will he please stand up," which he did. "Very well, you may sit down," said the Judge, adding that in all his years he'd never seen such a document and couldn't imagine anyone in his right senses buying a car under the terms of the document, concluding by saying that with the greatest possible regret he must give judgement in favour of the defendants. So that was the end of the 'home-made Guarantee' and from then on we operated with one professionally drafted.

Like all our competitors we were constantly searching for good used cars, preferably privately owned, often making quite long journeys out into the countryside to make inspections prior to buying. On one occasion when we had a really 'sticky' car that just wouldn't 'float away' we decided to advertise it from our house in Surrey giving no name or 'phone number — just the address. The result was quite startling — hordes of callers, none of them private buyers, all motor traders, most of whom we did business with anyway — and in the end the car did sell.

There was one rather enjoyable little interlude on the competition side at this time. With the Healey departed, we were enjoying open motoring with a really beautiful Low Chassis 4½ litre Invicta when, one day, a brochure arrived through the post announcing the formation of an Invicta Car Club, the leading light being Lord Ebury, also an Invicta Owner and a competitor in Club events and Hill Climbs. We sent in a subscription and a bit later got a 'phone call from Bill Ebury saying that the Club planned to field a team of six Low Chassis cars for the Six Hour Relay Race at Silverstone in a month's time, and would we come in as number six. I thanked him and said that though we'd gladly do anything we could to help, the car that we had was so nice that I really wasn't too keen to beat it round Silverstone and that in any case, lovely as it was, it wasn't by any means the fastest we'd had. Bill had the answer to that. "Well, why not put a call through to John Shutler. He's got a real 'goer' down at Burley Garage that he's selling for a customer. He's had it for a long time now and the owner's jumping up and down to sell it. Not a smart one but sporty, good mechanically — and a real flyer!" So I rang John, whom I knew quite well, and went down to try the car.

It turned out to be attractively priced and it really could go — easily the fastest I'd driven, and rather sporting with small light wings. Just the thing in fact. Bill had made the point that it would be number six in the team, not a reserve but the last car to carry the sash. It gave me a gorgeous evening run back from the New Forest to Weybridge and seemed to go even better when dusk fell and one had stopped for a pint.

Arriving at Silverstone on the day I found the Invicta team in a state of near chaos, with one car suffering from overheating, another from brake fade and a third with the strange malady of oil surge. Half an hour before the start of the race, the fourth car developed trouble and then Bill came rushing down to my bay with "Look Charles, I've got a problem with mine now. Could you possibly kick off first and do

An Austin Healey 100/4 owned by the Mortimers. Seen here with Jean driving at Goodwood in 1955 — — later to collect a spinning Buckler which appears to have already collected a 'ding' on the other side.

about half an hour, by which time we'll have at least two of the others ready.''

Anyone who ever ran in that race will know what fun it was. The main thing was the size and variety of the field, everything from 'C' Type Jaguars right down to Land Rovers and Volkswagen Beetles and every team consisting of six cars, rather like the Brighton road on a Sunday really. Not knowing an awful lot about the car, I took the precaution of filling it to the brim with fuel, oil and water and it was a good job that I did because, on the start line my 'briefing' from the Team Manager was that though they hoped to have another car operational in about half an hour's time, it might be slightly longer and could I keep going till I was shown a board saying 'In.' And also, would I have the sash free and in my hand to give to him so that he could drape it round the next to take over. I then had an absolutely great run for an hour and a half, dicing amongst the traffic before coming in having used gallons of fuel, oil and water — and some rubber as well. It was a hot day and I went straight to the bar tent with John Shutler, at that time the great expert on Invictas, having taking the precaution to refuel for the trip home and fill with oil and water. John's car was a Coupe but a fast one and though only pint-sized he was certainly the best Invicta driver there that day.

The fast 4½ which the author drove in the 6 hour Relay Race at Silverstone in 1954. Charles drove for a total of 2½ hours as the other members of the team kept on breaking down.

The course was great and I don't recall ever seeing it used again. Starting from the Pits it ran via Copse & Beckets, down the lefthand side of the long straight almost to Stowe where it did a 'U' turn round a marker barrel, running back up the straight to turn left at the top into the long straight on what is now the Club circuit and on down to Woodcote. Though John's drink was a quick one for he had work to do on two other cars, I thought mine could be leisurely and I was talking to Ken Wharton when the Team Manager burst in saying that they had such big troubles and could I go out immediately, "really for half an hour this time," adding that, at the moment, they hadn't a car in the race. So I did another forty minutes and was happy because with speeds so comparitively low one got such a marvellous view of the race and could enjoy all the action and drama. I had just one exciting moment. Someone had shed a sumpful of oil on the left-hander back on to the Club straight and the first time I hit it the old car really went for six, doing a great job in spreading what had at first been an oil-strewn area measurable in square feet to one barely measurable in square yards! I don't know where the Invicta team finished in that race. I know it didn't win but some-one in the bar was convinced that we had ranked as finishers.

It must have been around this time that things started to go wrong for me, first in a small way in business and then in a much more complex way personally. I spotted a lovely looking Phantom III Rolls razor edged sports saloon standing outside Guy Salmon's showroom in Thames Ditton and found that it was a 'trade in' that had arrived against a new car that morning. Guy, the straightest of dealers, told me he knew nothing about it, didn't want to, and suggested that I should take it and use it for the day and, if I wanted it, make an offer. I gave it a run of about sixty miles, stopping towards the

end to do odd bits of shopping, and made an offer which, in the end was accepted. Silly, really, I knew nothing of the P.III at that time, though I grew to know more later. Next morning, when I pressed the starter button, there was an awful graunching noise followed by silence and a second attempt produced the same result. I thought 'Jeepers, there must be a tooth missing from the flywheel ring' — and there I was! Later I found that the trouble only manifested itself when the engine was cold whereas I realised that Guy's tester would only have tried it when hot. I was in big trouble and knew it.

I took the car over to the Cystal Palace works of Jack Compton, a Rolls expert who had done work for me from time to time. I told him the symptoms and awaited his verdict breathlessly. Yes, I was right — and all he could do would be to replace the flywheel ring which would cost hundreds. But though that was the only full cure, he could put me in touch with someone in North London who could help me to the extent that a small and inexpensive modification would ensure that the starter would always work with the engine hot or cold — but it was a modidification which he, himself, was not prepared to make. So I went hotfoot and breathless to North London to meet an elderly, friendly, sympathetic and completely confident electrical engineer who staggered me with a quote of just five pounds and needed the car for no more than an hour. He explained the process to me. Unlike most other cars which were fitted with Bendix type starters operating on the 'spin and spiral throw in' principal the P.III starter motor had a straight spline so that, on pressing the starter button, the pinion slid without turning till it touched the flywheel ring teeth when a second phase would come into operation, pushing it more firmly into mesh. His modification would be to fit a second starter button low down beneath the dash which, when pressed, would bring the second phase into operation and effect a start. Groping below the dash as he spoke he said "Here, look, you're lucky. It's already been done. Your troubles are over.' It was a lesson learned that I never forgot — and a long time before I bought another P.III. Later, when the memory faded, I did buy quite a few and learned something else, from the same chap.

I bought a P.III up in Northampton, did a quick run down to London where I found myself in heavy traffic when, almost at once, the car boiled. Diverting at once to my friend, I found him just as confident as previously. "The thing with the P.III is that many of them were inexpertly laid up during the war years and though the cooling system may have been drained out, no attempt was made to clean out some of the less accessible water passages between the two blocks. If you're going to trade in P.III's always bear this in mind. On the run you've just done, the conditions were exactly those to cause boiling — a long, fast run followed by heavy, slow, traffic. Next time you go to buy a P.III made sure you take the owner with you when you try it, and ask him whether it's ever suffered from boiling. Nine times out

of ten he'll deny it with horror, so then reproduce these conditions in his presence — and if it boils you'll buy it much cheaper." I decided to stick to six cylinder Rolls from then on.

Talking of boiling reminds me of a trip northwards I once made with Edward Mills to buy an 8 litre Bentley sports saloon. Edward was once described to me as 'the last of the gentlemen traders' and he was. With a fresh rose in his button hole every day, he was always immaculate, urbane and a professional to his fingertips. He and I used to socialise and trade together and while I called him 'Edward the Elegant' he used to address me as 'Charles, dear boy'. Earlier in his trading life he'd been to some extent involved in the old Invicta company, later moving to London to join his friend John Fuelling in the small but select 'Knightsbridge Motors' firm dealing in only the best of good cars with the wealthiest and nicest of customers. He was, when I traded in London, the most expert, ethical and professional of all in his field. Buying or selling, his first concern was not to talk about the car but to find out all he could about the interest of the man with whom he

The Phantom III 12 cylinder Rolls Royce which was used as personal transport before being sold to the United States.

was dealing. If the man was a yachtsman, Edward could talk yachting, if a horseman, Edward had always loved horses, if a balloonist, that was something that Edward had always longed to do. People always love talking about their interests and are often short of listeners — and Edward was a marvellous listener if there was a deal in the offing. And that wasn't just a ploy, he really did become interested and was often invited down to stay at stately homes — and always, always, did the deal. He was also unflappable. On this occasion, the eight litre Bentley boiled the moment we got into the Hendon traffic. The radiator mascot had been removed and retained at the vendor's request, leaving a large hole in the top of the cap so that, when the 'brew up' occurred a vast fountain of boiling water shot fifteen or more feet up, scattering Hendon's shoppers in all directions. Ignoring their screams, Edward leaned well back in the driving seat, turning, smiling, to me with "D'you know, Charles, dear boy. I rather like that — unusual selling point — I think we'll keep that."

The Richards and Carr picture had changed since I joined, with more emphasis on new cars as they became available. We took on a sub-agency for Renaults and sold so many that we were honoured with a visit from one of the 'big pots' from Paris, leading to a move from our hole in the wall in Kinnerton Street to very grand showrooms in Lower Sloane Street, a move that we regretted almost from the moment we made it. On the motor racing side, Robin made a visit to the BBC to tell them how awful their motor racing broadcasts were, returning with the news that he'd been given the job himself. So this meant quite a bit of extra weekend showroom manning. Coupled with the fact that in Sloane Street a greater proportion of our clients were business people who really preferred to buy their new cars on their way home at the end of the day, meant later morning starts and later evenings as well.

As a motor racing enthusiast turned broadcaster, Robin was so successful that before long his services were required by the BBC virtually every weekend throughout the summer and, in the case of major races, for several days prior to the events, great for him and well deserved. But this did mean additional staffing at weekends which could

The Hooper bodied 8 litre Bentley was bought for resale but despite its size they grew very fond of it.

only be done by Dick and I, and though it wasn't by any means the sole cause, it did cause domestic strife and wasn't enjoyable so, all things considered and bearing in mind that Dick felt the same, it was at that time that we decided to negotiate the sale of Richards and Carr Ltd. Trading in Sloane Street was not nearly such fun as from our little slot in Kinnerton Street and I was tired and needed a break from selling cars and both my wife, Jean, and I felt that we wanted to move further out from London. So we moved from Webyridge nearer towards Guildford and that really ended my period of purely car dealing.

Really, that was the time to take a quite long holiday and though I did think about it, I opted, in the end for a fairly brief but absolutely great Continental break, thanks to my old friend James Tilling who suggested that as he was going to France to join John Bolster's involvement with the long-distance speedboat race on the Seine in Paris, it would be part of my education if I went as well. I had a suitable car at the time, a Freestone and Webb bodied sports saloon Rolls Phantom II Continental, originally owned by Kaye Don, registered GW1151, which gave me a great run down and back and an inkling of what Continental motoring must have been like in the early 1930's, that is to say, comfortable, fast but, at the rate of 10 miles per gallon, expensive. But Paris was lovely, the race amusing and at times quite exciting and, of course, any time spent with John and James, his foil, was always hilarious.

Back home and jobless I began to sort out my vast collection of motoring books and magazines, quickly deciding that half were too dry to read and would make a good base for a new start as a motoring bookdealer for, at the time, no one really seemed to have specialised in dealing in secondhand motoring literature though there were several who combined secondhand with mainly new. So with virtually no competition and by advertising that I would 'journey to buy and pay cash', I was once again back in business and 'wearing a new hat'. The idea of visiting their homes with pockets lined with cash appealed to vendors immediately and, initially my adverts produced such overwhelming response that it was hard to know in which direction to travel first. The collecting 'craze' had only just begun and, at the time, supply more than balanced demand so it was possible to buy books now classed as 'extremely rare' if not at two a penny, at least absurdly cheaply so that in almost no time, I realised I had the best secondhand stock of used motoring books in the country.

Feeling sure that others would follow, but not quite so sure that demand would speed up as fast as supply, I took a gamble, covered an enormous mileage in buying, met many delightful vendors, most of whom had enjoyed their motoring at the same time as I had, and finally decided that I really had become a secondhand bookdealer when I ran into the big snag that besets them all — shortage of space! Many times since then I was sure that I'd solved it before realising, as all bookdealers do, that it just isn't soluble. So I just forced on buying, slightly worried about it for about thirty years!

Thanks to John Morgan, Secretary of the B.A.R.C., I was invited to join the Club's Events Committee and later was promoted to the Council, whose first meeting I attended. I was appointed an Observer at Goodwood meetings and soon after one absolutely dreadful Nine Hour Race, on the same night as the Lynton and Lynmouth disaster, when our Observer's Box was blown over with all of us inside it, I was elevated to the positon of Deputy Chief Observer, one of my tasks being to go round the circuit between each race, collecting the Observers Reports for delivery back to Gordon Offord, the Chief. And I did quite a lot of this at Silverstone B.R.D.C. Meetings, including the Grand Prix. This turned out to be a rather eventful one because Jean and I had swopped cars for the day, she having my Peugeot while I took her Triumph Herald Coupe to Silverstone. When I got to Becketts, my Observer point, I found that my co-Observers were James Tilling, Duncan

Hamilton and other old mates including Tony Rolt. Duncan's Rolls Silver Cloud was parked near another similar car and while we were waiting for the programme to start, the driver of the other Cloud strolled over to ask Duncan how he liked his. "Well," he replied, "I came up with it a couple of days ago from the South of France, leaving at the same time as a heavily loaded baby Renault. By dint of hard driving, I did just manage to get to Paris first, but it was a close run thing and, right now, my feeling is that if anyone knows of a good Peugeot 403, I'd be quite interested in doing a level swop."

Nonsense of course but what he didn't know was the other driver was an official Rolls man who, appalled at such blasphemy asked if he was an 'experienced motorist'. "Fairly" said Duncan. "I've won the Le Mans 24 Hour Race a couple of times and usually do between a hundred and a hundred and fifty thousand miles a year." The 'victim' was appalled. "Well sir, I'm shocked to hear a driver of such experience express such an opinion on what is generally rated the finest example of light engineering in the world. My car has one or two modifications that yours lacks. Would you care to take it up the runway? Do what you like with it and let me know what you think." Off they went and what Duncan did with that car had to be seen to be believed; and when, finally, it was drifted, with its owner aboard, to an angle of roll that even its makers would have thought impossible, one wondered what the reaction would be but, to everyone's surprise, its owner turned out to be not only a courageous man but one with a great sense of humour. "Marvellous, almost impossible. The company will be delighted when they read my report. Thank you very much indeed Mr. Hamilton."

But it didn't turn out to be quite such a good day for me. When we all left in convoy after the last race, James was in Duncan's Silver Cloud, the skipper of Duncan's yacht in the Herald followed by Tony in his Jaguar round the main circuit, it became a race with the Herald as limit man. Off to a good start, we were rapidly overhauled by the Cloud which, instead of passing came closer ever closer behind, till we felt our rear bumper touched and all the power of the Cloud behind us applied. The Herald speedo went rapidly from seventy to eighty and then right off the clock at which point, much to the alarm of the skipper, it became unsteerable, luckily just as we reached Woodcote! Back home it seemed better to agree to Jean's view that we must have backed into something when parking than admit the real cause of a rather dented rear bumper.

New Directions

Our house move from Shere in Surrey to The Corner House at Ewhurst marked the end of my period in motor dealing and the start of the era of being a dealer in motoring literature, most of it early and all of it secondhand. At the time, most of my fellow dealers, though handling a certain amount of secondhand, specialised in new books, buying what secondhand stock they had when vendors brought it to them. Though I was myself a collector of early motoring literature, the collecting cult had then barely started. Initially, I built up stock by buying up what they had and at the same time advertising not only for early titles but also that I would visit the vendors' homes to do so; this produced massive reaction and resulted in much motoring. I kept my stock in a converted stable block situated in the garden of the house and, at the time it really seemed that while I was the only keen buyer, there were literally hundreds of willing sellers.

I advertised widely both in the U.K and overseas, mainly in the U.S.A. and, right from the start, the business grew until quite soon I found that I was the leading second-hand motor bookdealer in Europe; this state of affairs lasted for some twenty years. All of it was done from home and, of course, I had many visitors, both buyers and sellers, and I think really, that the building up of this business was one of the most interesting and inspiring periods of my life. It was, first, a change, different from what I had done previously, started at exactly the right time

when there were no problems of supply and at exactly the right time when the cult of secondhand motor book collecting became fashionable. I appreciated all these things and with them in mind, I worked like a Demon to make it work and was thrilled when it did. I quite liked the selling aspect but much preferred buying and always have, this was especially enjoyable in the summer when I would leave early in the morning, cover between three and four hundred miles, make up to half a dozen calls, all in a Mini, accompanied by my Boxer bitch, Judy, and arrive back loaded to the roof with books, just in time for dinner in the evening. I've never been one who professes not to enjoy motoring but have always enjoyed it and still do today. But the car must be good, even if small. I did have a bigger car, a Ford Cortina 1600E, but always bought using the Mini.

Selling? Initially, we issued about three or four booklists a year in the U.K. and overseas, advertising the fact in *Motor Sport;* but as the customers came flocking to us in droves, we stopped advertising to sell and only advertised ourselves as buyers, so the pot was always boiling. Quite soon we started receiving visits, at first from U.K. buyers and then, in their hundreds from buyers overseas. At this stage I took on staff, at first a wonderful secretary called Barbara Hain who soon knew the business as well as I did myself, virtually taking over the selling side, knowing the customers almost by their Christian names and releasing me from selling completely; when I was out buying, she handled all the selling and did the listing as well during the week although I usually took over selling at weekends. Originally, we had thought of exhibiting at Autojumbles but this turned out to be unnecessary though, having been at the first Beaulieu Autojumble, we always put on a big show for that because, selling apart, it was an opportunity to meet overseas customers old and new. We liked having visitors because, for one thing, it cut out a lot of postage and packing, almost the only aspect of the business neither of us liked.

But, initially, this also produced problems, the first of which was a visit from two tall and imposing gents whom I thought at first to be customers but who turned out to be Council officials wanting to know whether we had planning permission to use the site for anything except as a garage for horses. Fearful lest the 'phone should start ringing with clients ordering books, I steered them back to the house where Jean, scenting trouble, plied them at first with coffee and then, as the atmosphere unfroze, Scotch. Asked my profession, I was glad to have had time to consider that as we walked back up the garden and answered "Author and motoring historian, dealer in books also." All true. "Really! Do you write books or for magazines?" and when I said "Books" they asked if they could see one. *Brooklands and Beyond* worked wonders. "Brooklands" said one. "Did you go to Brooklands?" "Yes, I had a business in the Paddock there and raced bikes and cars at the track for ten years right up to the start of World War Two." "Well now. That's a coincidence. I was a police officer at Brooklands for over ten years. Did you ever meet Freddie Dixon, I wonder?" "Yes, Fred was a close friend. In fact he and his wife came to our wedding." It seemed unnecessary to say which wedding, the one in the 1940's or the second in the '60s. "Well now that's amazing. He always

used to stop at the gate and talk to me." We seemed to be home and dry though they did ask about planning permission, insisting that we should apply which we did — and got it. They were very nice and reasonable.

The second was initially worse but, again, alright in the end. The Income Tax Collector became convinced that, with our multiplicity of houses, we were dealing in them. They sent in a frightening claim and for some time just wouldn't believe the true story — but in the end they did; when faced with every detail of our rather ridiculous life stories, they enjoyed a good laugh and halved the claim. But, at the time, it was all rather time-consuming and concerning and it was good to be able to get on with bookdealing, and writing.

From then on, the bookselling business roared on, and the faster it went, the less time there was for selling big cars which, in any case, were becoming harder to find. Our last 'big' car deal pointed the way, for with good Rolls' becoming harder to find I tried restoring a huge late '20s-early '30s 'Double Six' Daimler, a Corsica bodied Drophead and one of the few with lowered chassis by Thompson & Taylor, more elegant than most Rolls' but a nightmare to restore and with no takers at the end of the long and costly restoration. To compensate for that I was delighted to receive a request from Lord Montagu for a quote for valuation of the contents of the library of the National Motor Museum at Beaulieu. A full day spent there only convinced me that so numerous and diverse were the contents that it really was impossible to give a proper quote but we sat down together and I put to him that one way of doing it would be for me to make two journeys a week from Ewhurst to Beaulieu, bringing with me my wonderful secretary, Barbara Hain, and that she and I would start working together at an agreed hourly rate for the two of us and continue either until the task was completed or until we were told 'enough was enough'. We did so for the next three months, somehow condensing six days a week into four, before being told that that really was enough. But a month later we got his 'go ahead' to complete, which we duly did. During the time we were at Beaulieu we managed to keep the sales and correspondence side of the bookselling side going but not the buying and by the time we had finished I had to spend the next two months 'out on the road.' That was no hardship for it was always the buying side and especially meeting and talking to the vendors, all of whom had a story to tell, that I enjoyed the most.

A typical case was a journey made to Norfolk to buy a rather large and nice collection of books from an elderly vendor. Large or small, every collection has the same basic make-up, a largish proportion of popular and less desirable books and a smaller one of scarcer and much more desirable classics. After checking the general condition, making sure that dust wrappers didn't cover up such faults as dampstained copies, 'Ex Library' copies missing pages or plates, I would divide each collection into two piles, those that one wanted and others less desirable. The latter always made a larger pile less easily sold and negotiations would then start. I would open by asking the vendor how much he aimed to get for his books, almost always getting the reply that he really had no idea of their value — almost never true. I would counter that by saying that if he had no idea, how would he know whether any offer I made would be fair; almost always this did reveal that, in fact, he had a pretty good idea. My next 'shot' in the game would be to say that, were I to buy his books, I would be paying him in cash, proving the point by putting the cash with the books on the table. This, more than anything else, nearly always caused a gleam in the eye.

Some vendors had memories of cars they had owned and would want to pick out books in which were illustrations of the cars. Even though one knew the contents of virtually every book, one had to be patient about this and show great interest because, to him, this was important. Having got this far I would say that I would make just one offer on which I wouldn't improve and, having done so, I would usually get either acceptance or refusal but sometimes a long discourse on why the offer was too low. One would feign interest in this, picking up the cash if one felt that the battle was going to be hard, quite often getting acceptance at this stage but, if not, would emphasise again that no higher offer would be forthcoming. After examining the whole lot once more, I would put them back in their respective piles while making the same offer for the smaller, desirable, pile which, really, was the pile that one had offered for in the first place. This nearly always brought instant acceptance.

Many vendors were male, elderly and obviously lonely with a lot of experience of past motoring so that, for them, the occasion was social and, however badly one wanted to press on to the next call, one just had to listen to their reminiscences even when the deal had been done. At times like this, coffee, tea or something harder would flow while the floodgates opened. On the Norfolk occasion, the vendor asked whether I dealt in anything other than books, and as usual, I said I would buy almost anything I liked, either for myself or for resale. This produced a large telescope, obviously quite early and in nice condition but not my kind of thing. Strongly pressed to make an offer, I tried to avoid it but in the end offered £15 which was instantly accepted.

At that time Jean, my wife, was a fringe dealer in antiques and although she had no luck with it at antique fairs, she had a visit one day from a dealer who, after making odd small buys from her stock, asked if she had any nautical instruments. I produced my telescope and after examining it carefully, the chap asked the price. I said I was looking for an offer and after another close examination he came out with "How do you feel about £200?" I said I could sell it for that and we did a deal. I felt unhappy about that, rang the vendor and told him, his reaction being "Jolly good luck to you" and after I'd said I would send him another £85 we had quite a 'battle in reverse' before compromising at £45, very unusual because subsequently he put several old friends in touch and I bought their collections as well.

On another occasion, when going to see a big collection of books down in the New Forest, we found that the vendor had a quite smart and original 1929 Austin Seven for sale. Jean came with me that time in the Citroen 'ID19' I had at the time and, finding that the Seven still had a current tax disc, we bought it as well as the books and set off for home. We stopped for a drink and a sandwich ten miles down the road. I hadn't driven a 'Seven' for years and had quite forgotten how appallingly pedestrian they were so, to save time, suggested that we towed it home behind the Citroen. Not too keen on the idea despite being an expert 'tower', she replied impishly "I'll promise you one thing: if we do, it'll be the fastest and most exciting tow of your life." So, in the end, we didn't. But with the possibility of a breakdown and since she had shopping to do in Alresford and Four Marks we compromised with the arrangement that while I would continue to run non stop, she would tie a handkerchief on the door handle of the Citroen when stopped, which I would remove as I passed and return when later she caught me up. I don't recall how long the journey took — it seemed a lifetime! But the client who later bought the car said it was one of the liveliest and best he'd known!

Our buying side became quite highly organised with a large map of England, Scotland and Wales mounted on a board on the office wall with red coloured pins stuck in denoting our mailing list clients and white for vendors of book collections so that when, once a week I went off to buy, there were nearly always three and sometimes more grouped to visit on the same day. We never set off anywhere without having, first a list of not only the books but also their editions and a description of their condition and whether with or without dust wrappers and, if possible, some idea of the price hoped for. As one who has always enjoyed buying rather than selling, the 'buy' day each week was a highlight often leaving home, in the summer, at six o'clock in the morning or earlier and returning loaded to the gun-whales with new stock. Inevitably there were sometimes failures and disappointments, by far the worst of which was a trip I made up to Scotland. We had a call from a Scotsman whose name, fortunately, I can't remember, offering a large collection of books which included a full bound run of *Motor Sport* right from its start. Calling me constantly by my Christian name, I came to think he knew me but however often we requested a full list he always refused, saying that he hadn't time to make one, so big was the collection. In the end I misguidedly made the journey, stopping overnight just south of Glasgow and making the trip in a Mark 9 Jaguar to be sure of having enough space for the load. His opening remark was "One thing I must tell you. My son didn't want me to sell the *Motor Sport* so I've given them to him this morning." The collection, mostly good titles in awful condition, was in the grotty little office of his marine engineering business, eighteen books in all whereas he had clearly said 'eighty at least' on the phone and all on one small shelf, leaning heavily to the left so that all the spines were twisted. Making a swift exit without comment of any sort, I gunned the Mark 9 southwards, glad to stop and give a lift to a young R.A.F. sergeant who looked a bit glum, and was, because having made the same journey from the south in order to finalise marriage plans with his betrothed, had had a blistering row with her and had left to go back before she surfaced. With some experience of that sort of problem, I urged him to 'phone her before taking him too far south, which at first he refused to do though I could see that by the time we reached Gretna Green, stopping for coffee, he was weakening. In the cafe, I said "Right, I'll get the coffees. You go and 'phone your bird," which he did, returning with his face wreathed in smiles and the news that they were back to 'square one'; could he have my name and address because his fiancee wanted to write and thank me? In fact, she did and they were married in due course, sent me an invitation to the wedding and kept in touch constantly for years. So it wasn't at all, as it might have been, a wasted day!

Another comic one involved a library offered by a publican down in Kent. Lovely pub, nice man, superb collection: the only snag being that as it was the only day that week that I could visit him, the deal had to be done during opening hours. Sitting in his comfortable private lounge, we were miles apart on price at the end of the first round and very little closer at the end of the second. He produced a bottle of very good wine which we shared while ramming home to me his view that the condition of his books, in every way far ahead of the average, must merit a highish price and really it couldn't be denied. So, in the end, and with the bottle now empty, I bought them. As I finished loading them into the car he came out carrying a large box. "Here, take these. I've never liked them. Sorry to have given you rather a hard time" — and rushed backed to his bar. I opened the box and found a full run of *Automobile Year* from Volume One and a slightly smaller one of

Autocourse, together more valuable than those I'd already bought. Almost tottering back to the bar, I said "Look, I can't take those, they're valuable." "Are they? Not to me. I don't like those large format things. I never read them and they're space takers." I put money on the bar and said "Can we talk it over in your lounge — over another bottle" and he pushed the money back. "Good idea but on me and I'm still not taking anything for them." Back we went to the lounge, had a go at the second bottle though, in the end, he just wouldn't take another sou.

It was at this period that, when going to London to look at a 25-30hp Rolls, I saw in a Mews garage GO51, one of the original Fox & Nichol Talbot '105' Sports racing team cars, only slightly showing its age but still elegant, very rare and, above all, for sale quite reasonably. From memory, I thought there's been only four of these, three four-seaters, GO51, 52 and 53 and a fourth, not at first road registered but a Brooklands single-seater which, when the team disbanded, was retained by Arthur Fox, a near neighbour and family friend, fitted with a saloon body, registered APF999 and used by him for years as daily transport.

The purchase of GO51 started a chain reaction when only a short time later I came across APF999 and bought that as well. I not only remembered the cars so well but knew Lord Essendon who, as the then Honourable Brian Lewis, was the team's leading driver and remembered the others among them Tim Rose Richards and Saunders Davies. It had always seemed to me that whereas the Bentley racing teams of the 1920s and '30s had had far more publicity than they deserved, the Talbots had had almost none despite being, in some ways, even more successful. So I began to think about writing up their racing history in a book and, thanks to Arthur Fox, had already got some way along the road with it, even to the point of

The author at Silverstone with two of the famous Fox & Nicholls Talbots. The car on the left is the original single seater rebodied as a saloon and on the right the better known GO 15. Left to right 'Dunlop Mac' (in overalls), Charles Mortimer, Edward Mills and Lord Essendon who drove the car in the 1931 Mille Miglia.

having a meeting with Georges Roesch, the cars' designer, whom I'd found just as prickly and brittle as Arthur had been charming and helpful.

Both the Talbots seemed good mechanically and both smart with their new paintwork in the original colours. The British Racing Driver's Club were putting on a parade of Historic Racing Cars at the Grand Prix Meeting at Silverstone and Desmond Scannell wanted both to run in it with their original drivers, saying that he would look after the driver aspect and the Club would underwrite the cost of bringing them to Silverstone, if I would guarantee their presence.

On the morning, and well ahead of schedule, I located both Brian and Arthur in the bar fraternising and reminiscing with others of their era. Both seemed in excellent form and, having told them when their presence on the start line would be required, I went back to supervise the unloading and starting up of the cars. Both Edward Mills and 'Dunlop Mac' were there and it was good that they were because, ten minutes before the start there was still no sign of our 'drivers'. Dear Arthur Fox arrived with the news that Brian would 'be coming shortly' and while Edward drove GO51 to the line

I took the saloon. Five minutes to go and still no sign of Brian. Secretary Des Scannell was getting edgy: "This was always the problem — getting Brian organised. If he doesn't make it you'd better drive it Charles, after all it's your car." But with almost seconds to go, Brian did, immaculate as ever in raincoat and brown Trilby hat and rolled up umbrella. Sorry to be late. Got kept. Now where's this motorcar. What did you say it was, a Lagonda?"

"No, Brian, a Talbot — and you drove it successfully in the Mille Miglia thirty years ago." "Good Lord, yes. One of the old Fox & Nichol cars. Damn good cars. What's that old heap that Arthur's trying to get into over there?" "It's the old single-seater that Arthur had re-bodied when the team disbanded. You drove that regularly. In fact, you and John Cobb shared it and finished well up at around 100 in the 500 Mile Race — mid thirties."

That's right, damned uncomfortable too. Had to have a block of wood nailed to the floor to wedge one's foot under to prevent getting chucked out. But I'll tell you one interesting thing about that. It went right through that race without a tyre change. Quite remarkable at the time for a car of that

129

weight and speed."

As they left the line, Mac strolled over. "Amazing how he always says that even now. 'Fiddle' and I changed both backs when the car refilled at half distance. By the time Brian had handed over, the original wheels — and both jacks — were over the counter and half way back to our van. But it wasn't John who drove with him that year, it was Saunders Davies. The 'Big Six' Bentley which Jack Dunfee and Cyril Paul shared won the race, 1931 I think, at about 118mph and Brian and Saunders Davies were second at just under 113mph. It was said afterwards that if they hadn't changed rears they might have won, but that was nonsense. By the time they'd changed drivers and refilled we were half way back to our van. But he did say, after the race, how remarkable it was that they'd got through without changing the rears. I just smiled and let him think it."

It was later that day that I met Anthony Blight for the first time. We'd spoken on the 'phone previously and I knew him as the most knowledgeable and mono minded 'Talbotiste' of all, already including at least one of the team cars in his fleet. He was desperately keen to meet Roesch whom he'd found un-cooperative so, without telling Roesch, I asked him out to lunch where he found Anthony as well. We lunched at the Carlton Tower Hotel and within the first ten minutes I realised that, difficult as I found Roesch, he and Anthony were so much on a beam that they hardly knew I was there.

That lunch turned out to be, in a sense, historic. My interest in the Fox and Nichol Talbots centred mainly round their racing performances, especially when compared with those of the almost over-publicised Bentley successes and bearing in mind the difference in engine size, three litres in the case of the Talbots and four and a half and six and a half litres of the Bentleys. This, rather than the design aspect, was obviously

of much less interest to Roesch in our previous meetings and during the threesome lunch we had that day, it became obvious to me that if anyone were to write a book on the Talbot it should be Anthony rather than I. After Roesch's departure, I made him a present of what I had already written which, in the end, turned out to be only a fraction of the end product: *Georges Roesch and the Invincible Talbot*. Only a short time later he and I met again and, this time, he bought from me not only the two Fox and Nichol Team cars but also what remained of BGH23, the most successful of the similar but not identical Pass and Joyce team Talbots.

Though, till then, I had only had experience of the pre-Rolls period 6½ and 8 litre Bentleys, I had one more of each of these, the 6½ being the rather historic sports four-seater owned by Stanley Sedgwick which, driven by Gerry Crozier during Stanley's ownership, had covered over a hundred miles in less than an hour, a lovely car, faster than any of the others I'd owned but essentially a performer and rather stark and it was through Edward Mills that, in the end, I sold it. The last 8 litre was a long chassis four-door sports saloon which gave me about six month's motoring, the most memorable trip of all being one to Brighton with James Tilling, following John Bolster's early Panhard on its umpteenth successful Brighton run. Not really an ideal Brighton tender car and by the time we got there, I'd had enough of it and it was James who drove us home.

At this time, the early 1960s, I'd had almost no experience of the Rolls era Bentleys but replaced the 'Eight' with a low mileage four and a quarter which gave me good, completely trouble-free motoring till a buyer showed up, when I replaced it with a pristine 1939, razor-edged bodied '4¼' with overdrive and carosserie by Freestone and Webb. Once again, a buyer emerged, in a way disappointing because that was a car that I really would like to have owned for longer — but it was always the ones that one would have liked to have kept that floated away soonest. The next was very unusual, a 1935 '3½', rebodied by Abbots of Farnham with an attractive and ingenious 2/4 seater open sports body, the emphasis being on two rather than four seats with a rear hinged tail, the top of which lifted to reveal two rather smaller seats. This came by courtesy of Johnny Marshal outside whose garage at Shepperton I first saw it.

Had it not been for the fact that one particular Mark 6 Bentley came up out of the blue, I think I would have held on the the Abbot bodied '3½' but, this time, the opportunity was too good to miss. There was a story behind it, too, which went right back to the late 1930s. At that time, a Mr. Mcleod purchased a new '4½' overdrive, less body, and designed and fitted a body so different to any other that, on seeing it, one either hated or adored it — and I adored it. It wasn't for sale on either of the two occasions I saw it and even if it had been, it would have been doubtful if I could have afforded it. Externally, the only three things recognisable as Bentley were the radiator, the bonnet and the wheels. A very close-coupled, angular, fully razor-edged body with the starkest possible flared wings, no rear luggage boot but in its place a fully exposed large capacity fuel tank shaped as those fitted to the pre 1931 sports racing team cars, at that time gave it the appearance of half 'modern' and half 'vintage'. The first time I set eyes on it, it was in a traffic block in Berkeley Street in London's, even then, heavy traffic and the second was years later when, after having being sold overseas, it returned to England for a full overhaul and refit. I knew nothing of its conception or origin at that time but, years later, mentioned it to my friend Edward Mills of Knightsbridge Motors who, of course, knew all about it and told me not only about Mr. Mcleod but also that the bodywork had been carried out by H. J. Mulliner to his design.

So imagine my astonishment when, after the war and when passing Jack Olding's showroom, there stood a Mark 6 Bentley which had been given identical treatment by the same owner, the only difference being

The author always wishes he had kept this one a little longer. A 3½ litre Bentley with coachwork by Abbotts of Farnham, it had space in the tail for 2 more passengers.

that a small angular rear boot replaced the slab fuel tank of the pre-war car. By now, the car which was absolutely a 'one-off' had come to be known as the Post-War 'Mulliner Lightweight' and was in process of its first change of ownership so was still priced at a figure to which i couldn't go. It had, by now, had a changed registration number and was LMU576, its original H1 being retained by Mr. Mcleod. In due course it sold and I had to wait another three years before it came up again, this time at a price I could manage though, at the time, I doubted whether, when the time came to part with it, I would ever succeed in finding a buyer.

The further I drove the Mark 6 'Mulliner Lightweight' the less I worried about that for, of all the cars, it was the one I loved best and still would like to own again even though I know I never will. It was no faster than a 'standard steel' Mark 6 of its period. Its appeal to me was the way it did what it did, its improved road holding, its better acceleration and the fact that, compared with the standard product, it always felt smaller, the faster one drove it, and sometimes almost 'Mini like'. It was the one road car that I've always loved above all others — the one whose appeal never died. If cars had souls, I think the feeling was mutual because when, years later, it was offered to me again in part exchange for a 1952 'small boot big bore standard' steel Mark 6, I clinched the deal so quickly that the vendor seemed almost alarmed at the ease with which the deal had been concluded.

I had another good spell of ownership, sold it again and took it back again, part exchanged for a 1953 Bentley 'R' Type with manual gearbox resolving that, this time I really would keep it for all time. But in the end the 'dealer instinct' came bubbling up again though, wrongly, I'd grown to feel that our relationship was such that it would keep 'coming home'; that time it didn't.

Despite the vast mileage I covered with it, it never once gave even small trouble and we did many long runs together including one with the Bentley Drivers Club to their annual speed trials held in Belgium, near Antwerp. The Club was keen for us to attend though LMU576 and I didn't know at the time that one of their reasons was that there should be a sprinkling of Mark 6s among the gathering to act as towing cars home for competitors unfortunate enough to throw con rods or break crankshafts during their runs. In fact it was I who ran into trouble that time, meeting eight litre owner 'Jumbo' Goddard who, after a spell away on safari, was crying out for the bright lights of Antwerp; so together with Bart Loyens we went out 'on the town' ending in a nightclub that supplied us with such vast quantities of 'hooch' that, though it seemed palatable at the time, floored me — and 'Jumbo' as well — the sole survivor being Loyens who sobered us both next morning by presenting us with our share of the bill! So, deciding that we liked each other's company better than the bright lights, LMU576 and I made our way slowly and ruefully home!

Around this period, a new and, for some time, consuming interest entered my life following a talk I had with an old Brooklands friend, Francis Beart. He and I had gone to Brooklands at the same time and though our interest in motorcycles and racing were different, we had for years remained old friends. At Brooklands, my interests were in racing the machinery rather in maintaining it and seeking more speed. Francis' interests were the opposite and it was the technical side, especially development and tuning that really appealed to him, so much so that when I switched from racing bikes to cars we moved in different circles even though, at the track, we would often lunch together in the Paddock canteen. We lost touch completely during the war when I joined the Macklin group and he veered away towards aero engine development.

Motorcycle engine tuning and development was still his great interest after the war and our paths crossed again at car race meetings, mainly at Goodwood and Silverstone at the time when Stirling Moss was becoming a leading light in the 500cc car racing era. At that time most of the leading 'half litre' drivers were Cooper-mounted and JAP-engine powered, but though the JAP speedway engine was excellent for sprints, the overhead camshaft Manx Norton was far better and more reliable for races and when our first meeting in this area came, Francis was already closely involved with Moss in tuning and maintaining his engines. Other 500cc drivers veered from JAP to Norton power and though Francis already had a vast clientele of Norton-mounted motorcycle racing customers, he somehow found time to become involved in the car side as well, even to the extent of running a car of his own which Stirling drove. However, this new aspect meant that, as a sponsor and entrant in motorcycle racing, he'd had to cut out short circuit racing and concentrate on just two big races each year, the Manx Grand Prix and the Tourist Trophy races in the Isle of Man. The Manx G.P. of course was the amateur version of the T.T. and once a rider won the Manx he was no longer eligible to compete in it but had to go to the T.T. But, as a sponsor/entrant Francis could run bikes, with different riders in both.

It was during a lunch we had together one day at Goodwood that Francis asked me if I missed the racing and when I said I did, he said "Then why not buy a couple of bikes, a '350' and a '500', pick yourself a young 'up and coming' boy to ride them, let me prepare and maintain them and come over and do the T.T. in June and the Manx in September. I'm signed up with Shell and can put you in touch with their Competition Manager, Lew Ellis, who could give you a list of the brighter unsponsored youngsters.

Then come over for the Manx with me in September, spend some time out on the course for practice early each morning, pick your runner from the list Lew gives you, get the bikes now so that I can prepare them this winter, and do both races next year." I didn't say I'd think about it, just said I would and we lunched with Lew three days later — and signed with Shell. Lew was a marvellous character and knew of our Brooklands involvement. He said: "Here's the list then. Study their riding form first. Then when you've picked one, let me know and I'll tell you whether to go on with it. Pick a second and a third choice as well because today's riders are a different breed to your old mates and you won't like all of them. That's quite important because, obviously you'll spend quite a lot of time with the chap and if you find you can't stand him, you're on a short ride to nowhere." So I spent a lot of time out on the course in September, picked a youngster called Griff Jenkins, spent more time hanging around his outfit in the paddock and went back to Lew. He said "Fine, you couldn't do better. He's a nice lad, quiet, and I agree with what you say about his riding."

I met Griff a week later in the bar of the Bear at Esher. We talked and he was as pleased as I with the prospect of the Manx and perhaps the T.T. a year later. But there was one snag. He was doing all the short races on his own bike as well: would that be alright? It was with me but I felt I'd really like to be involved in those also so I went to 'phone Francis. "Short circuits, Charles. No, don't have anything to do with them. All the leaders are lunatics with no idea of how to treat a machine, no mechanical knowledge or desire to acquire any. If you want to wreck a machine, run it on short circuits." So our equipe became a new five hundred Manx Norton, a three fifty 7R AJS, that had done only one Isle of Man race, both for major races only, with Griff's five hundred Norton and a not so smart but very quick 7R that I bought for short circuits. Griff and his brother Alf were to transport in their Ford Thames van the short circuit bikes and maintain them and Francis to tune, prepare and maintain the 'major race' ones.

Francis' big Norton, ridden by Joe Dunphy, won the Senior Manx Grand Prix that year. Griff had many short circuit wins and places the next year and crowned the season by winning the Senior Manx on my five hundred at a then, record average of 96mph, but through being far too anxious to please early in the season, had many accidents, one or two of them being bad, both for him and the machinery.

All this led to another activity because when, one day, we were all down at Brands Hatch for testing, Joe came in complaining not only about the number of riders on the track but also some who didn't know what they were doing. "What's really needed" he said "Is a proper school, like the car people have." Francis looked at me. "How would you feel about that? Phil Kettle and I could maintain the machinery. It would have to be 250cc two-stroke production racers. Simple to maintain, no valves to get bent and light enough not to damage too much when 'thrown down the road'. So, together, we started the first Motor Cycle Racing School ever to be held in the U.K. or, as far as we knew, anywhere else — 'The Beart-Mortimer Bike Racing School'.

It wasn't easy. The big problem was that at car racing schools, a pupil was first taken round the circuit for several laps in a two-seater, driven by the instructor who showed him the line and told him what to do, something that couldn't be done with a bike. He then went out in a single-seater, following the instructor in the two-seater, and later, on his own. But that was a problem that had to be surmounted — and it was. Francis undertook to fix up contracts for machinery, accessory, fuel and oil supplies while my

part centred round planning and organisation. My first visit was to consult John Cooper who then ran the Cooper Racing school. His easy style made light of it. "Well there are only about three rules really. First, never let a customer near the machinery till you've got his money in your hand because no one likes paying for something that he's broken. Second make it clear, always, that you're the headmaster, you're in charge and what you say goes. And third, as headmaster, cultivate an air of calmness and authority. Never run. Running destroys confidence. If it's a crash that's the emergency, and the customer is actually under the machinery which is burning, a gentle jog trot with a fire extinguisher, and preferably with a 'boys will be boys' sort of smile, that's ideal. It gives confidence to the other customers and implies 'action' even though that sort of accident is an everyday occurrence." And that was all I could get from him.

Francis tied up a first class contract with Bert Greeves for, initially, six new 250cc Greeves 'Silverstone' Production Racers, and with Lew Ellis for supplies of fuel and oil. Someone came up with supplies of racing leathers, gloves, boots and crash hats — and we were nearly in business.

Or so we thought. Before doing anything we'd done some market research to make sure that aspiring youngsters would use such a service and, with this established, we went ahead to cover the legal aspects, insurance of the machinery and personal accident for the customers and, of course which circuits would co-operate. We planned to use Brands Hatch, with Silverstone, Mallory and Oulton Parks, Snetterton and Cadwell Park coming in later. We particularly didn't apply to Brands first because we feared a refusal whereas if we could say that we were already doing it elsewhere, the chances seemed better. So we went up to Cadwell, took its owner, Ernie Wilkinson, out to lunch and got an immediate and enthusiastic acceptance. No insurance company would cover the damage to the machinery and, with hindsight, how right they were. But we were able to get good personal accident cover for the riders and for ourselves as a result of any claim that might be made against the School.

We still didn't ask the Brands management but just joined in the open motorcycle practice days, Wednesdays and Saturdays, at first with just a handful of customers and, week by week, adding more. It must have been six months or so before the management twigged it and, even when they did, they gave us great co-operation, mainly on our past good records at nearly all the other circuits. Six more new machines followed which meant additional transport, at first our older son Charles' Ford Thames van, already used for transporting his own racing machinery but this, after thousands of miles use on the Continent, was so awful to drive that I bought a new one from John Coombs, fitted it with a ball hitch and added a double-axle Rice horsebox which meant that we could now transport four racers in each van and five more in the trailer. Griff became Chief Instructor with Chas as his deputy and from that moment on we had more business than we could possibly cope with.

Initially, the charge to the customers was £1 per lap. Training sessions consisted of a minimum of ten laps, the first five following an instructor, who then waved the pack on and joined it to study form from the tail end. The greatest number of customers we ever had on a training session was twelve with two instructors, starting with one at the front and the other following and, at half distance, one in the middle. Later, we ran advanced sessions for the more promising and intrepid and, later still, very advanced ones. We had tremendous co-operation from the big stars of the day, many of whom did stints as instructors, including well-known names like Barry Sheene, Bill Ivy, Rex Butcher, Ron Chandler and others. Poor old Chas inherited the task of machine cleaning, basic maintenance and instructing and quite a lot of office work as well, for each machine had a number and a log book of its running history including any accidents in which it had been involved, mileage covered since overhaul, and any other information concerning it; that job alone was a time consumer. Some pupils were much harder on machinery than others and at one stage we even had two bikes set up for clients who consistently over revved the engines; the rev counters were converted to read two thousand revs per minute higher than their engines were really doing, just so that such customers could feel that they were really getting value for money!

It all added up to a very busy week. For me, it was bookselling on Monday with Chas cleaning and servicing the previous Saturday's machinery. Tuesday, bookselling while Chas loaded the transport with Wednesday's School session. Wednesday, all hands to the circuit. Thursday as Monday. Friday as Tuesday and so on. It varied, of course if we were taking the School 'away from home' to circuits such as Cadwell, Oulton or Snetterton, each of which meant an overnight stop.

For me van ownership was a new experience and while none of the riders seemed to take much interest in theirs, I had mine fitted out with all mod cons, including special seats, steering wheel, carpets and instrumentation so that, in the end, the cab was more comfortable than many popular type cars. The old Ford forward control Thames was an excellent vehicle and though I didn't know, at the time, how lucky I was, mine was one of the first with a four speed gearbox. Lucky because when fully loaded and with a full load in the trailer, third gear was golden even on motorways where I spent more time in third than I'd thought possible. If the motorway wasn't crowded and was reasonably unhilly, I used to have a change from the slow to the middle lane but gave this up when Chas, Barry or Paul Smart used to creep up unnoticed in the slow lane, lean out and deal the side of my van an almighty bang with their fists. This never failed to make me jump and wonder what part of my load had collapsed and fallen on to the rest. One really had to have eyes in the back of one's head to keep up with them at times and life was never short of laughs.

I still recall one awful day when we stopped at a remote little cafe inside which was a blackboard giving the prices of refreshments. Everything was priced. Ham sandwiches so much a round, beef so much, cheese — the lot. The cafe had a little putting ground and this also was priced at so much a round. Chas, Paul and Ron Eldridge were in the convoy that day and Ron was the first to give his order, a coffee and a round of ham sandwiches, Paul tea and cheese sandwiches and Chas a glass of milk and a slice of cake. Everything was set up when Paul said "Oh, I didn't know they'd got milk" — after his tea, of course, had come. Then followed an idiot conversation whereby they all changed their orders, each saying that he'd do a swop but none agreeing the charges on the basis that, as they hadn't had what they'd ordered there shouldn't be a charge. At the end of it all, Chas said "Look Ron, putting sandwiches. Haven't seen them for years. Can I change my cake for a round of putting sandwiches," so both Ron and Paul wanted putting sandwiches as well. By this time I'd finished and was about to get back in my van, but not before the proprietor came out with "You know sir, if I couldn't see that you're not that sort of man, I would have assessed you as connected with a mental institution." I didn't blame him.

Since Shell were supplying the School with fuel, the vans carried their current advert 'Super Shell with I.C.A.' which stood for 'Internal Combusion Additive'. The boys always sought 'Attended Service' filling stations so that, the moment the pumps began to roll, they could say "Just a minute, hang on. We do want Super Shell — but without 'I.C.A'. We don't think it's good for the valves." Obviously an impossible order but they always insisted that most filling stations would filter out the 'I.C.A.' through oiled silk. Stupid but it did cause laughs.

We ran the School for nearly three years and, in that time had more than two thousand boys through it. During that time, we had only two serious accidents, the first at Oulton Park where a pupil suffered serious leg injuries, the second at Brands Hatch where, after a fall, another's heartbeat stopped twice on the way to hospital even though, next morning, he was sitting up cheerfully in bed, asking when he could have his next ride! But we knew that the time had come to call it a day, feeling that we had almost certainly saved some lives, had saved nearly all our pupils money avoiding mistakes and had still never had a fatality. Chas and Paul went on to become brilliant riders and Barry to be a World Champion even though he'd been a valued Instructor and helper rather than a pupil. And I wanted more time for bookdealing.

At this rather late stage of the game, three more cars, two of them really bought for re-sale and one intended as an 'own smoker', came along and became 'my own' covering quite large mileages. The first was one of the last Minor 1000s turned out, a model that we'd owned earlier but hadn't kept because, at the time, it was in short supply and, therefore retailable easily. We covered nearly 10,000 miles in this, low mileage and beautifully maintained little car and were still in love with it when it finally 'floated away'. Minor 1000s seem to have quite a strong appeal for elderly gents enjoying the evenings of their lives perhaps because, unlike the box-like shape of their successor, the Mini in all its forms, the Minor does look like their conception of a car. Two eminent owners concluded their motoring careers with them to my knowledge, the first being Land Record Speed breaker, George Eyston, and the second W. O. Bentley who, when we lived in Surrey, we used to see doing his domestic shopping in Cranleigh.

The second, sandwiched between our first and second Minis, was perhaps the most attractively and elegantly bodied of all small cars of its time, the little rear engined Fiat '85' Coupe. A lovely looking little car and quite a good performer and cheap to run. Our example, like the Minor, had been well maintained but had two snags. The first was that, despite its past good history, we kept up a constant battle against body rust during all the time we owned it. The second was that, being a small car, one tended to compare it with a Mini and, where roadholding was concerned, it fell far short. Our '850' Coupe gave me quite a big fright quite soon after we bought it. One grows to know every bend of one's local roads and we had one that had an apparently slow left-hand bend that could, in fact, be taken much faster in a Mini. Where the road itself joined the grass verge, there was quite a deep gully into which one could 'hook' the nearside front wheel of a Mini so as to get round at undiminished speed. The first time this was tried with the Fiat, it didn't work out, the wheel going in perfectly but suddenly becoming 'unhooked' and losing adhesion completely. This didn't surprise a fellow '850' Coupe owner at all, this theory being that that was quite in character and easily cured by leaving a heavy weight in the forward-sited luggage compartment — and a large suitcase filled to bursting with unsaleable magazines certainly bore out his theory!

The third of these cars, owned in the late 1960s to mid '70s, was a beautifully maintained, 'one owner' 1953 Rolls Royce 'Silver Dawn', standard steel bodied and with manual gearchange — a car that one really should have hung on to, and did for longer than most. In retrospect, I think that younger people's classification of Rolls Royces as 'an old man's car' may be right but, at the time we had the 'Dawn' we were already in character. Either one is a lover of Rolls Royce or one isn't but having owned every type and horsepower for over a period of twenty years, from 1933 to 1953, I confess to being the former. If, within that period, I had to pick one above all the others, it would be the last of the 1930s 40/50hp Continentals, an absolutely fabulous car, streets ahead of any Bentley of its period with, as a very close second, the 'Dawn'. In the period that I had the P.II 'Continental' its size wasn't the snag that it would be now but, today even the 'Dawn' would feel too big at times when parking.

The disposal of the Racing School was a relief and, at first, gave me time to sit down and think before setting off in another direction. The running of the School and the constant commitment of Wednesday and Saturday sessions at the circuits, apart from the office work involved and time spent in bookdealing, seemed somehow to have taken its toll. For the first time in my life I really felt tired. It was Jean who summed it up. She said "Has it ever occurred to you that you're not as young as you were and that, at sixty five, you really ought to be thinking about retirement instead of fighting the clock through every single minute of every day. How about selling the bookselling thing, too, and retiring in Devon which we've always loved. We might even have a little pub down there and do bed and breakfast for all your old customers?" I'd never looked at it that way — it didn't sound bad at all. I was also surprised to find that though my interest in most aspects of motoring hadn't waned, I no longer yearned for big, fast cars for driving conditions had changed. One couldn't leave a Rolls or Bentley outside the pub after dark without finding oneself minus a mascot, and if one wanted to park a big 'un it meant a long search for a berth. So I began to think about lively small 'uns.

Two things then brought about a change. The first was the invitation to undertake the valuation of the Beaulieu Motor Museum library which was, to me, a tremendous compliment, so big, in fact, that once the task was completed, I really did want to opt out of bookselling then and there. The other was that, in the past year, I'd had several intimations from customers of the bookselling business that I might like to consider partnership. One of the first came from Eoin Young — a bit too early because, at the time, I'd not really decided what to do and needed to think about it longer and, by the time I'd done that, Eoin had alrady set up on his own. Then, quite a bit later, I had the same suggestion from Eric Thompson, a friend from the early post-war racing days and by that time I certainly had taken a decision. I knew I didn't want to go on running the thing on my own because the character of the business had changed. In the early days I'd had a regular stream of visitors, some to browse and others to buy, for at that time I really had no competition. But with overseas interest catching up with and passing interest in the U.K., my job, apart from buying which I always preferred, had become a 'sender out of quotes' and 'packer up of parcels' — and very insular.

I wasn't happy about a partnership either for, having run the thing solo for countless years, I felt that a partner would almost certainly want to make changes and that if I disagreed with his ideas, good as they probably would have been, that could be difficult. So I told Eric my thoughts, adding that I did now feel ready to sell outright. It was in 1979 that he bought it and though, through making a wrong decision in retiring

down in Devon we did have problems, I never regretted the decision to sell.

By that time, both Jean and I wanted to make a move even though it wasn't until eighteen months later that we did so. Initially, I spent some months writing a book, *The Constant Search,* on the subject of the literature of motoring. Then I had a visit from Eoin who said that, if Eric had no objections, would I feel like reorganising his (Eoin's) bookselling business so with Eric's agreement, I went over to have a look at the problem which turned out to be massive, mainly from the point of view of storage. Surprisingly, the problem wasn't lack of storage space so much as the available space being used to the best advantage, for Eoin, a skilled and prolific buyer hadn't really been too interested in the storage aspect, for which I didn't blame him because storage is a constant and dreary problem for all booksellers. But, in this case, it was a big problem because, for months, any books bought would go on to shelves or laid where they fell, in boxes all over the vast central floor. We lunched together and he asked me what I thought. I said what I thought, that the problem was massive, would take one person three months to solve and could only be done by complete 'degutting' and by the purchase and careful siting of additional shelving. His reply to that was "When can you start?" and my answer was "Tomorrow," which I did and enjoyed helping him for the next eighteen months! The whole of that time was thoroughly enjoyable and he was absolutely marvellous to work with. Initially, things became lost in the melee. Valuable things, the loss of which would have driven me crazy. But he never seemed to worry but always seemed confident that that they would turn up, which they always did — sometimes at his house! His sense of humour was acute and I always recall the time when the book problem was nearly sorted out and we'd moved on to the storage of a vast accumulation of motoring pictures. I said I thought the best way would be to hang them on the walls. His reply was "Magic. I'll get you some steps." By the end of the week we'd run out of wall space and when he next came in, I said "Eoin, we've got a little problem with these pictures." Putting down half a dozen huge boxes filled with his 'Buys' he walked off with "No good bellyaching at me, Grandad. You were the one who buggered it up." On another occasion, a very windy day, he wanted a huge motoring poster taken out into daylight so that he could photograph it. "Just hold it up straight. I'll take the picture." Impossible. It just kept twisting and curling up. After the fourth attempt he looked at me with "Tell me, what else are you good at?" It was an amusing and enjoyable stint.

Then we moved to Devon. We'd always enjoyed spring, summer and autumn holidays there. But we'd never tried a winter one. We were lucky, at first in having two glorious summers. But the winters are different down there. Everything seems to be closed and it rains continuously and it was only when we were fairly well into the second winter that we were both surprised to find how much we disliked it, Jean feeling cut off from our children and grandchildren and I finding a total lack of motoring interest or activity. So, at their suggestion, we moved again from Devon to the Warwickhsire-Northamptonshire borders. The older one becomes, the harder it is to adjust to changes and, though years younger than I, it did take Jean a bit longer than I to achieve it. Easier for me because, apart from being only ten miles from Silverstone, I found that, almost all the year round, there were Autojumbles and markets, north, south, east and west — so I jumped back into harness and restarted a business buying and selling anything, apart from books, that could be classified as Motoring Art. Mascots, badges, photographs, pictures, prints, trophies and awards, it was all there.

Devoid of a mailing list, I advertised my resurrection and, one by one, all my old customers returned — and many new ones. It was great, and I didn't miss any of the 'Classics'. The Ford 1600E was followed by a Triumph Vitesse saloon, quite a sparkling performer at the time but lacking the roadholding of the 1600E which led to another one, one of the last to be turned out. Then came the 'Mini' era. First a new '1000' which did good service, followed by another the same. Then a 'Clubman', a 1275 and two Mini Coopers, both sparkling performers for their size, neither too smooth enginewise and both rather noisy. How lucky I've been to have owned those wonderful old cars at a time when one could use them day to day and really enjoy them. Though I wouldn't want any of them today, I find the V.S.C.C. meetings at Silverstone nostalgic and inspiring and try never to miss one. And thanks to our sons, I'm kept well up to date with the Grand Prix scene which, though so much changed, is fascinating though, as a rule, we tend to go to the practice periods rather than to the Grand Prix race itself.

To their great credit the Committee of the British Racing Driver's Club made antiquities like myself life members some years ago which means a comfortable Clubhouse with a balcony from which to watch and, for good measure, an excellent restaurant and bar where one can meet and talk to old friends while enjoying the racing. Another superb Silverstone meeting is the Truck Grand Prix and a short time ago, I rang my old friend George Abecassis, who lives just down the road and with whom I have a monthly lunch date, to suggest that we made our next rendezvous the B.R.D.C. Suite for lunch and to watch Truck Grand Prix practice. "Trucks, Charlie. Who wants to watch bloody trucks? I said "You do, or rather you will, when you see them lapping at the same speed, with a chicane, as you

Nostalgic re-union in the 1980's. Driving Bob Wood's Invicta at a Brooklands re-union meeting.

did in the works Aston DB2 without chicane'' and almost disbelievingly, he came, and agreed.

Other good things can happen. A year ago, at the Brooklands Reunion, Bob Roberts generously offered me a drive round the Byfleet Banking at the wheel of his Bugatti Type 43. An absolutely marvellous gesture which — who knows? — I might have accepted if it hadn't been for the fact that, recognised by the current young owner of a beautiful Low Chassis '4½' Invicta, I'd snapped up his offer to drive that. Yes, there's plenty to enjoy still. Motoring? Yes and no. In the course of my motor ephemera purveying business, I do still cover a big annual mileage, mainly to buy. I don't agree with contemporaries who say that there's no longer any pleasure to be had from motoring.

A long run with a really early morning start still holds the same old magic and, at that time of the morning, even motorways can be enjoyable before the 'Yuppies' get out and about.

Motorways? They're magic. There's nothing wrong with them apart from the space they take and some of the half-wits who use them, driving cars far faster than they can handle. People of my age should bear in mind, no matter how excellent they think their driving to be, that whether they realise it or not, their reactions aren't what they once were. In this context I always recall seeing an elderly gent, driving a Minor 1000 and obviously lost in London's traffic. Car and taxi drivers were yelling abuse at him and, as I passed, I recognised him and wondered what would they have felt if they'd known they were shouting at George Eyston, holder of the World Land Speed Record in 1938 at a speed of 357mph. Now that I'm the same age as he was then, I do try to keep out of the way. My current Mini 1000, standard except for wider wheels and tyres, will register over eighty downhill and with a bit of a gale behind it but on motorways it's happier in the slow lane, jogging along at between sixty and sixty five among the less fast 'camions'. It takes a bit longer to get there but, in the end one does.

Sixty years of motoring in a number of different forms and, businesswise, always connected with it! How lucky I am to have discovered another aspect of it: motoring art in the form of mascots, badges and ephemera. The early phases of building up a new business are so often the most enjoyable — and I do hope I can have a bit more of it still.

It's amusing, too, to reflect that the first motor cars to arrive on the scene only beat me to it by twenty years, and consider my grandfather's strongly held view that if man ever tried to exceed a hundred miles an hour in a car, his blood would congeal and he'd die!

Regrets? Not too many really. I wish I'd worked harder at school and during the start of my time in the car trade and thereby learned more about the technical side. Though I can't bring myself to regret the years I spent at Brooklands, it would have been better not to have had quite such an obsession with racing. But, my wife and family apart, my greatest good fortune had been to have lived through such a wonderful era of motoring — a time when there was room for all road users to use their cars, to park them and not to have to worry whether when, returning to them, mascot or badges had been stolen, or worse, to find that some freak had run a screwdriver down the side. One of the greatest aspects of late 1920s — early '30s motoring was to see how the early light cars, the Austin Sevens and Morris Minors, opened up a new vista for millions who, till then, had never known the freedom of the road. There was no aspect of envy anywhere. Arriving at Brooklands in one's Austin Seven or Ten, and finding Sir Malcolm Campbell's 38/250 Mercedes parked nearby, one's first reaction was to stroll over and have a good look at it — not to vandalise it or swipe it's 'Three Pointed

Charles Mortimer's favourite road car. He owned it 3 times. The controversial H. J. Mulliner Mulliner lightweight Mark 6 Bentley. More acceleration and better road holding than the standard car. Charles also liked the look of it.

Star' mascot.

Having been lucky enough to own, drive and trade in so many of the great cars of my period, at a time when one could enjoy them as daily transport, there are few that I'd want to own again today. Given the chance I could settle for either the H. J. Mulliner Lightweight Bentley Mark 6 or a 4½ Litre Low Chassis Invicta as 'fun' cars, a rather swish Mini for every day use and a Rolls Royce 'Silver Dawn' with manual gearbox and standard bodywork for state occasions. I wouldn't want a later one because it seems to me that almost all 'prestige' type cars get bigger, the later they are. If my choice could include a 'bread and butter' car of the past, I think it would have to be a Ford Cortina 1600E. Even if I had them all, most of my motoring would be in the Mini, so no regrets at all there!

The last car that I sold when regarding myself as purely a car trader was a Gurney Nutting razor-edged-bodied Rolls Phantom III. A beautiful car which I sold to a Scotsman, a difficult man who not only hammered me on price but also wanted the price to include delivery to Edinburgh which meant, perhaps, standing the additional outlay for forty gallons of fuel. He called, inspected and tried the car, saying he'd make a firm decision next morning. He 'phoned from Edinburgh around eleven o'clock next morning, confirming the deal provided the car could be on his doorstep within twenty four hours, which it was. His promise to pay cash was kept — with one proviso — that the tank should be refilled again before I returned by train. He had me over a barrel and knew it, but I was glad to be out of the car-dealing business and always regarded him as the first of a new breed of customers, rather than the last of the old! I don't recall the fuel tank capacity of a P.III but I suppose that, with two 'buckshee' fills, he could have won to the extent of about eighty gallons; around £160 at today's prices.

Reverting to 'regrets': yes, one fairly big one. It would have been far better had we moved from Surrey to where we are now, on the Northampton-Warwickshire borders instead of assessing ourselves as retirement material and pottering around for two years in Devon. But here we are at last with our family and grandchildren all within easy reach and, Thank Heaven, the wheels of commerce once again turning merrily — and Silverstone with all its memories and excitements almost within walking distance!

And best of all, of course, I'm still sharing a roof with the same wife I wed more than forty years ago, when our temperaments were just as diverse then as they are now. I believe they do say that opposites attract — but I can only speak for myself.

Memories? One mustn't dwell on them. There's nothing worse than to hear a geriatric begin a phrase with the words "I well remember", indicating a long, often dull and tedious reminisce. But they do have a habit of cropping up and can occasionally be interesting. When exhibiting at one of the Classic Car Shows recently, I sold something — I think it was a car mascot — to a customer of about my own age. He continued to browse over the stock, noticed our business card and said "Charles Mortimer? Are you the Charles Mortimer who used to race bikes at Brooklands? If so, you and I once had a big dice which I won by a whisker." I said "Remind me" and he went on "It was in 1939. We were both running in a three lap outer circuit race. I don't think we'd ever met actually but I knew you by name and you might even have known me. You were riding Francis Beart's three fifty Norton and sidecar and had some start from my five hundred Rudge." I said "Your name is Owen Greenwood" and he said "How on earth can you remember that?" I replied "Very easily. You won it by a hundredth of a second, and my first words to Francis were "Where the hell did that bloody man

Greenwood come from?'' We both enjoyed a good laugh.

Another, even stranger one, also in a market, this year. Again, sparked by our trade card, a customer said "I think you and I met once, way back in the early thirties. You were just becoming known at Brooklands and were dealing in big 'hard-to-sell' cars. I wonder if you can remember buying a big open Sports four-seater '36/220' Mercedes up in Norfolk? I said I did and he went on "Having bought the car, you then stopped at a small roadside filling station which had two pumps, both hand operated. Twenty gallons went in, with you holding the spout and the proprietor doing the winding of the handle. It was the biggest fill of a car he'd ever done at the time. Cars and photography were my interests then and I photographed the fill and subsequently the picture, which I think was captioned 'A Record Fill', appeared in a local paper. I do still have that picture and, if you'd like me to, I'll post it to you as a present." And, marvellous chap, he did and I now have it framed. It's a bit sobering though, as he said, to note that at the time and based on petrol at around two shillings (10 pence) a gallon, the fill would have cost £2 whereas at today's rate of around £2 a gallon, one would have to fork out around £40! But that's progress isn't it? Or is it?

It's great for aged Brooklands habitues to read about the interest that still surrounds the old track even though one does come across a discordant note sometimes. I read a letter in *Motor Sport* recently saying how dull and awful Brooklands and everything to do with it must have been. I showed the letter to another driver of my era whose comment was "Poor sap. He thinks he's living. He doesn't know the meaning of the word."